FOR ORGANS, PIANOS & ELECTRONIC KEYBOARDS

E-Z PLAY TODAY 6

SONGS OF THE **BEATLES**

3RD EDITION

Photo © Getty Images / Roger Viollet Collection

ISBN 978-1-5400-3449-6

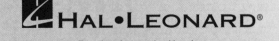

Visit Hal Leonard Online at
www.HalLeonard.com

Contact Us:
Hal Leonard
7777 West Bluemound Road
Milwaukee, WI 53213
Email: info@halleonard.com

In Europe contact:
Hal Leonard Europe Limited
42 Wigmore Street
Marylebone, London, W1U 2RN
Email: info@halleonardeurope.com

In Australia contact:
Hal Leonard Australia Pty. Ltd.
4 Lentara Court
Cheltenham, Victoria, 3192 Australia
Email: info@halleonard.com.au

All My Loving

Registration 9
Rhythm: Rock

Words and Music by John Lennon
and Paul McCartney

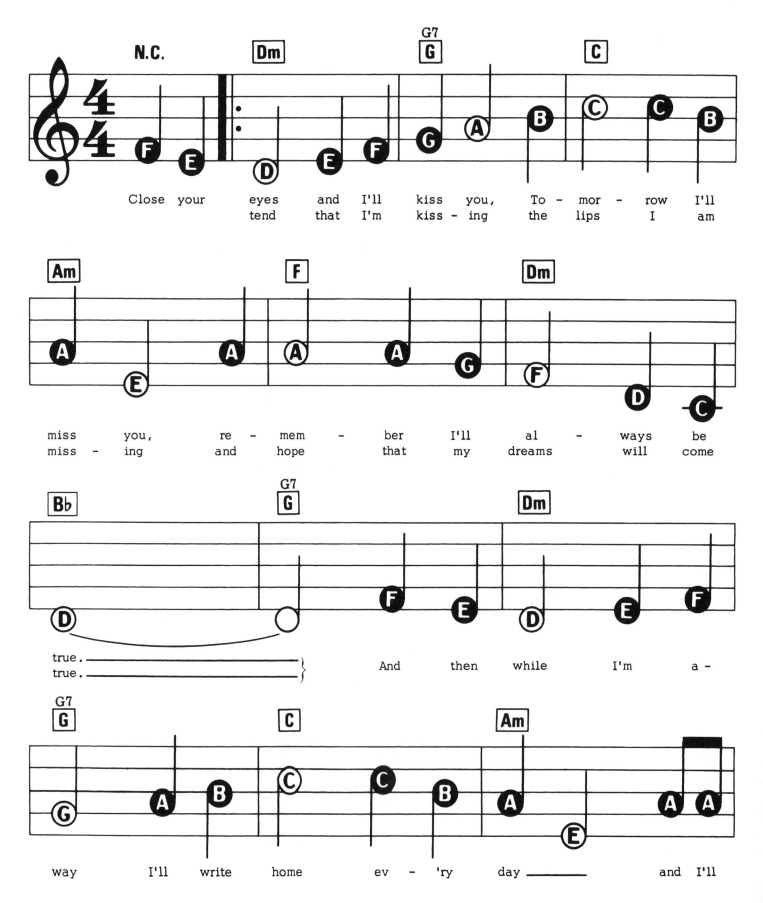

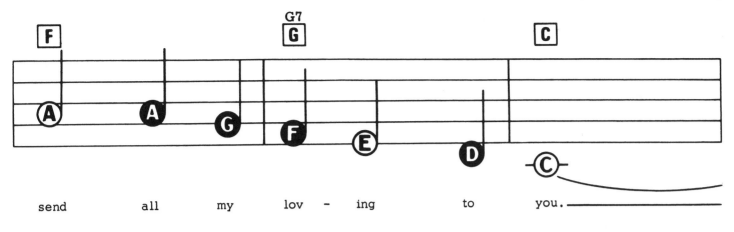

send all my lov - ing to you._____

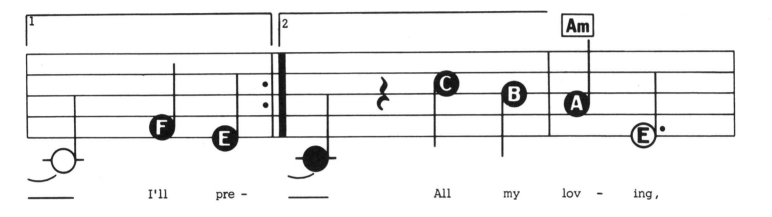

_____ I'll pre - ____ All my lov - ing,

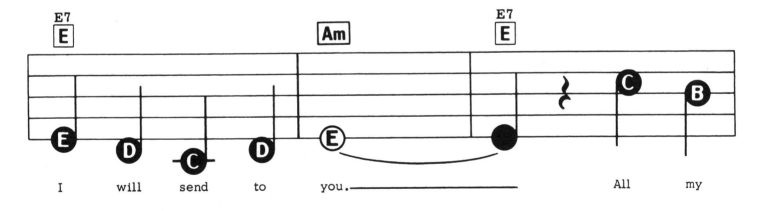

I will send to you._____ All my

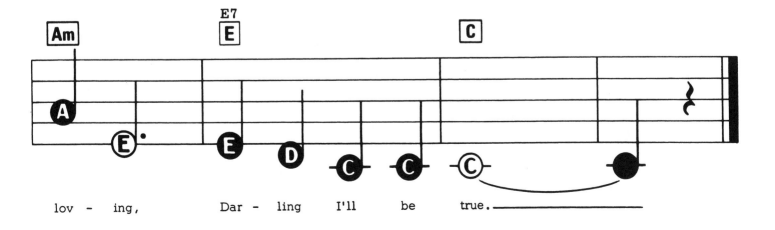

lov - ing, Dar - ling I'll be true._____

And I Love Her

Registration 8
Rhythm: Rock or Jazz Rock

Words and Music by John Lennon
and Paul McCartney

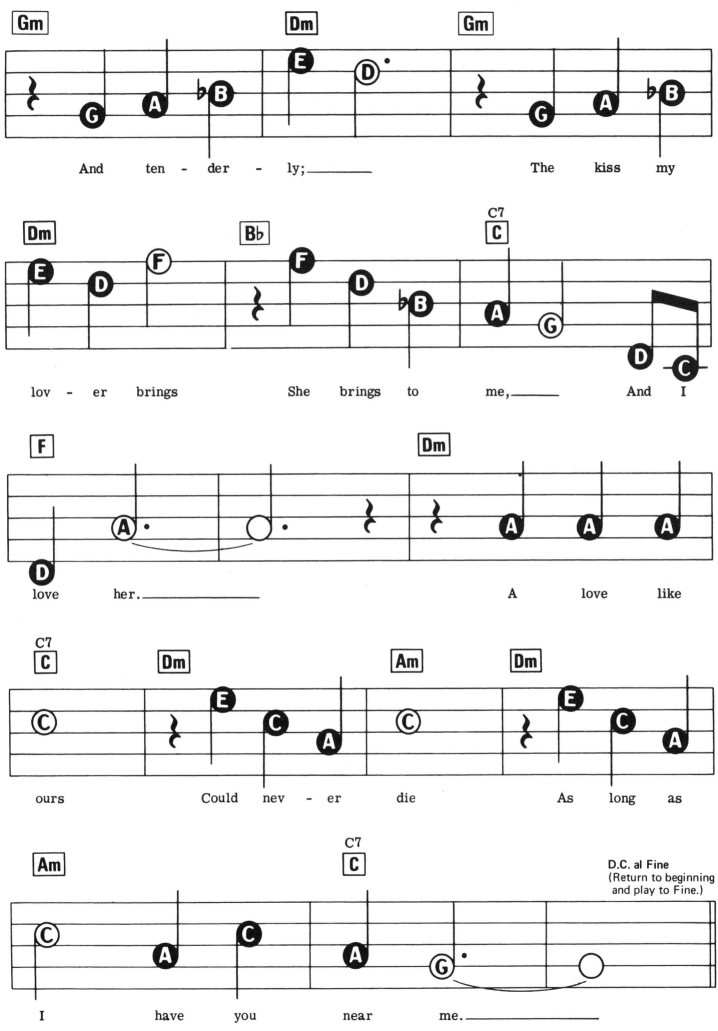

Back in the U.S.S.R.

Registration 4
Rhythm: Rock or Jazz Rock

Words and Music by John Lennon
and Paul McCartney

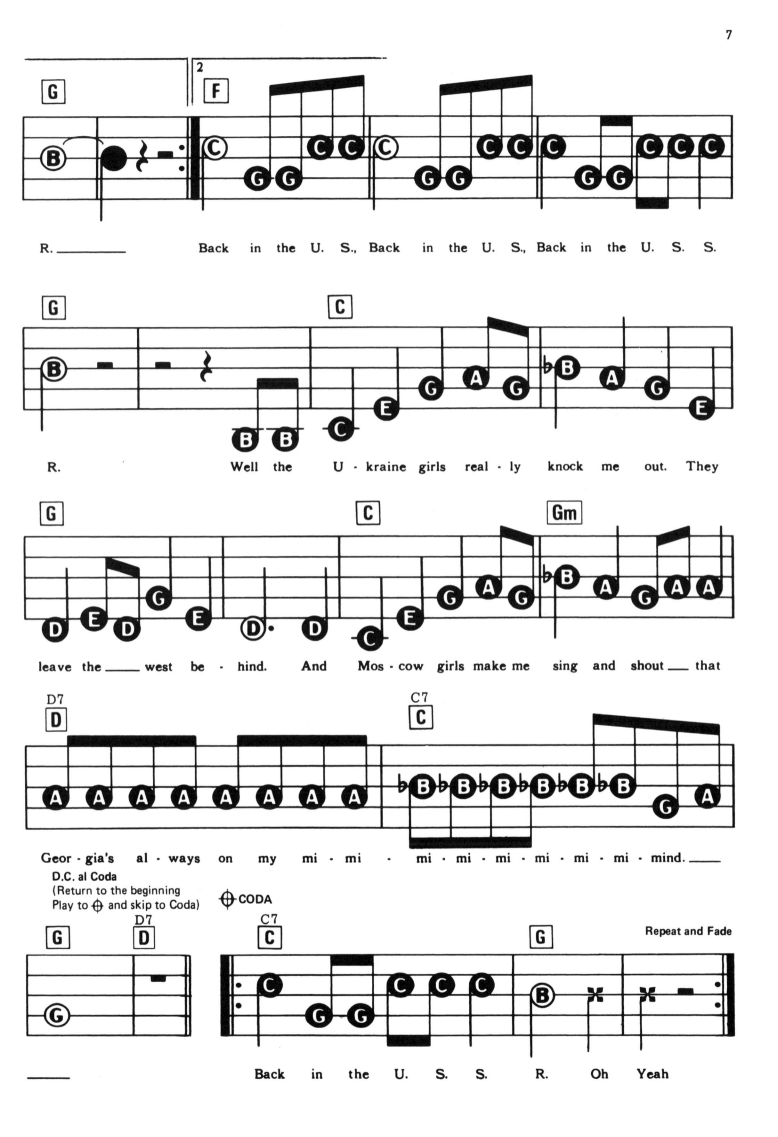

R. _____ Back in the U. S., Back in the U. S., Back in the U. S. S.

R. Well the U · kraine girls real · ly knock me out. They

leave the _____ west be · hind. And Mos · cow girls make me sing and shout ___ that

Geor · gia's al · ways on my mi · mi · mi · mi · mi · mi · mi · mi · mind. ____

D.C. al Coda
(Return to the beginning
Play to ⊕ and skip to Coda)

⊕ **CODA**

Repeat and Fade

_____ Back in the U. S. S. R. Oh Yeah

Can't Buy Me Love

Registration 1
Rhythm: Rock

Words and Music by John Lennon
and Paul McCartney

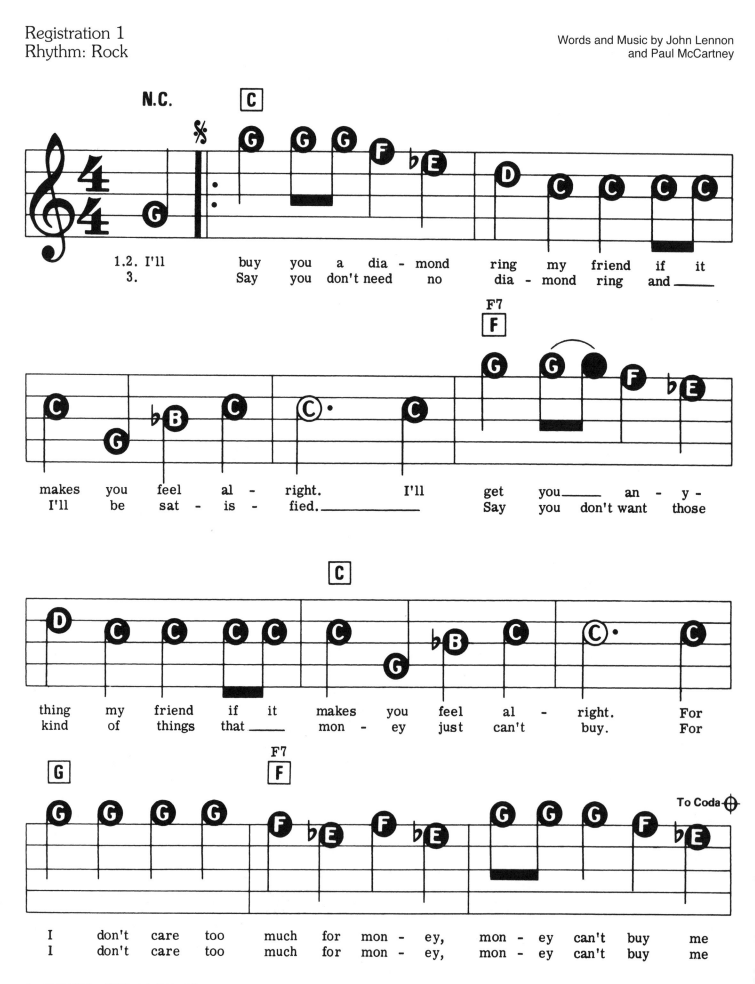

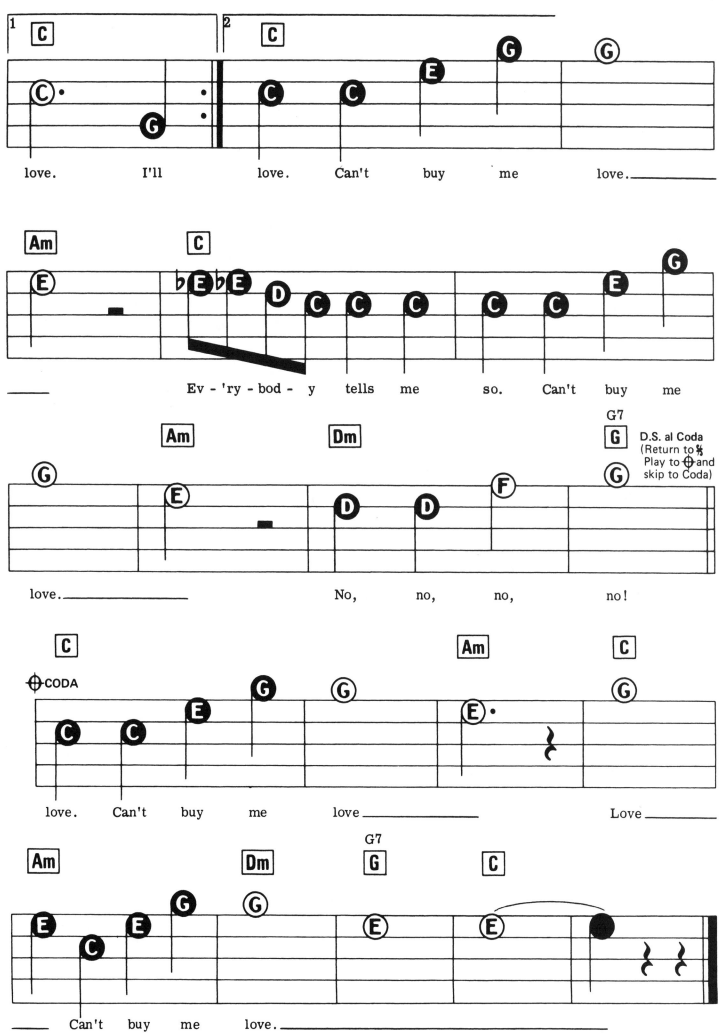

Come Together

Registration 9
Rhythm: Rock

Words and Music by John Lennon
and Paul McCartney

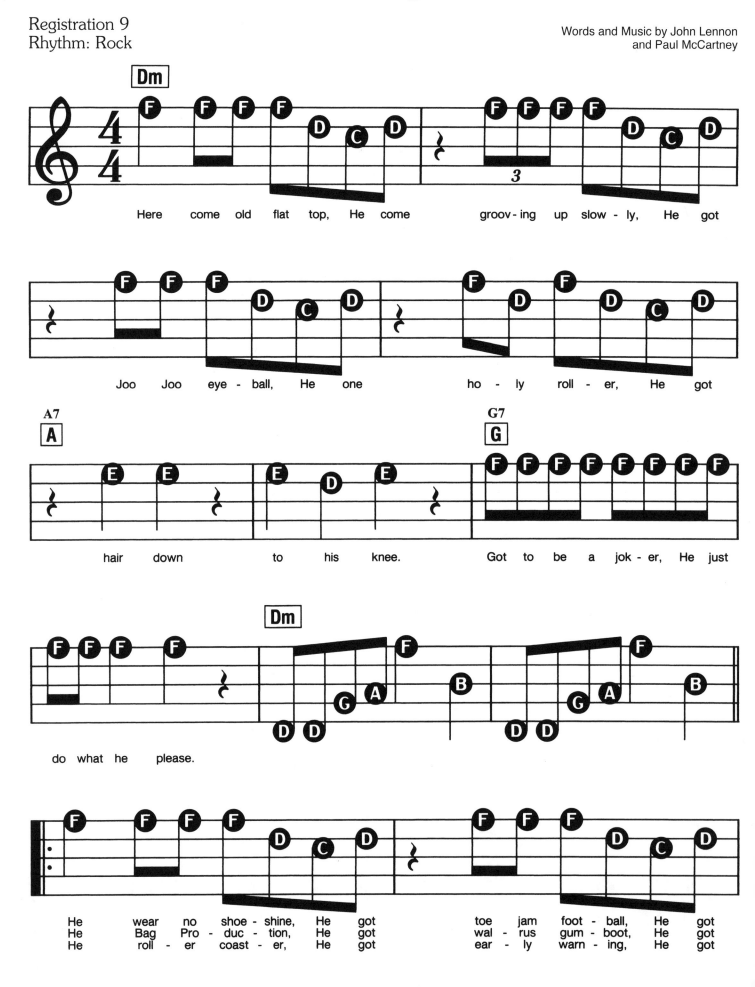

11

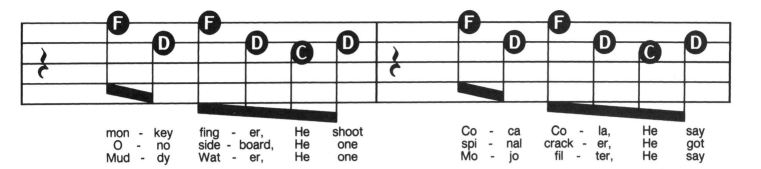

mon - key fing - er, He shoot
O - no side - board, He one
Mud - dy Wat - er, He one

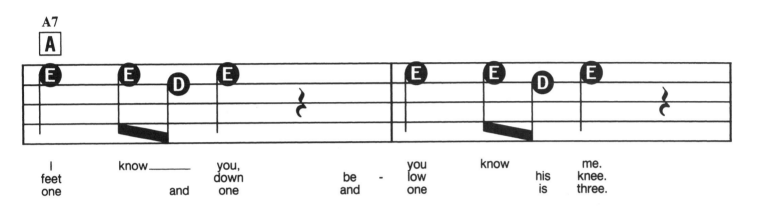

A7
A

I know___ you, you know me.
feet one and one down be - low know his knee.
one and one be and one is three.

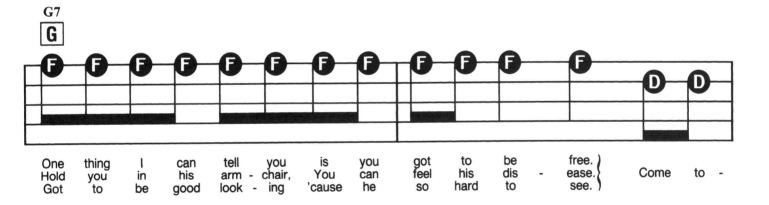

G7
G

One thing I can tell you is you got to be free.
Hold you in his arm - chair, You can feel his dis - ease.
Got to be good look - ing 'cause he can so hard to see.

Come to -

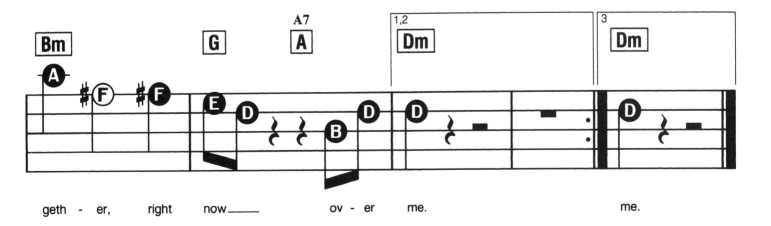

Bm   **G**   **A7**   **1,2**   **3**
                   A   **Dm**   **Dm**

geth - er, right now___ ov - er me.   me.

Day Tripper

Registration 2
Rhythm: Rock or Disco

Words and Music by John Lennon
and Paul McCartney

Got a good rea - son   for tak - ing the ea - sy way
Tried to please ____ her   she on - ly played one night

out.   Got a good   rea - son   for
stands.   Tried ____ to   please her,   she

tak - ing the   ea - sy way out now.   She was a
on - ly played one   night stands. now.   She was a

day ____   trip - per,   One way tick - et,   Yeh. ____
day ____   trip - per,   Sun - day driv - er,   Yeh. ____

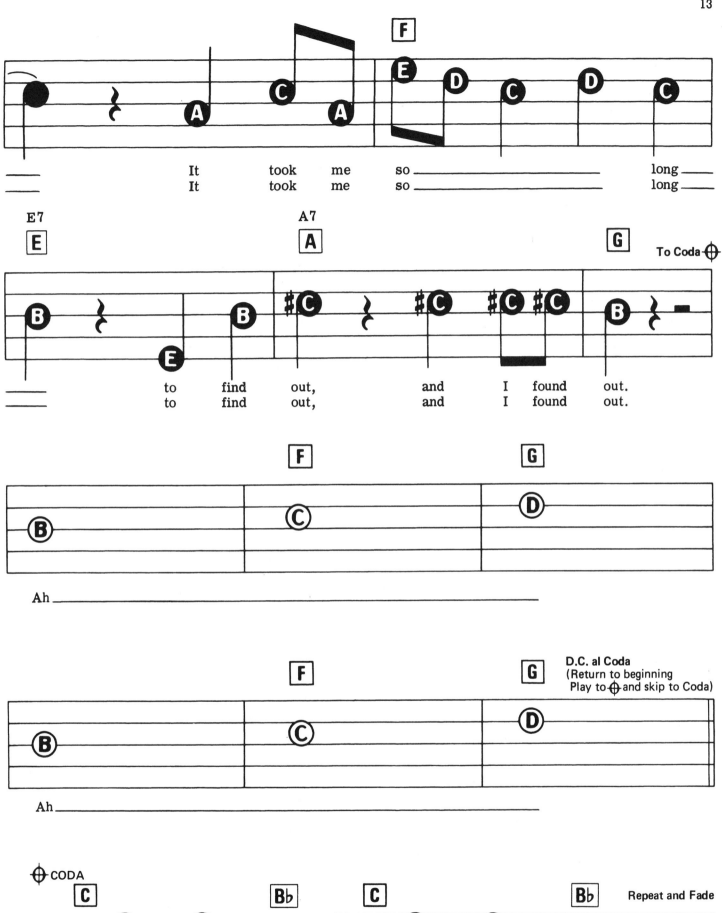

It took me so _____ long _____
It took me so _____ long _____

E7 **A7** To Coda ⊕

to find out, and I found out.
to find find out, and I found out.

F **G**

Ah _____

F **G** D.C. al Coda
(Return to beginning
Play to ⊕ and skip to Coda)

Ah _____

⊕ CODA

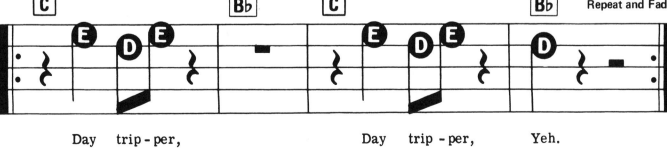

C **B♭** **C** **B♭** Repeat and Fade

Day trip-per, Day trip-per, Yeh.

Eleanor Rigby

Registration 9
Rhythm: Rock

Words and Music by John Lennon
and Paul McCartney

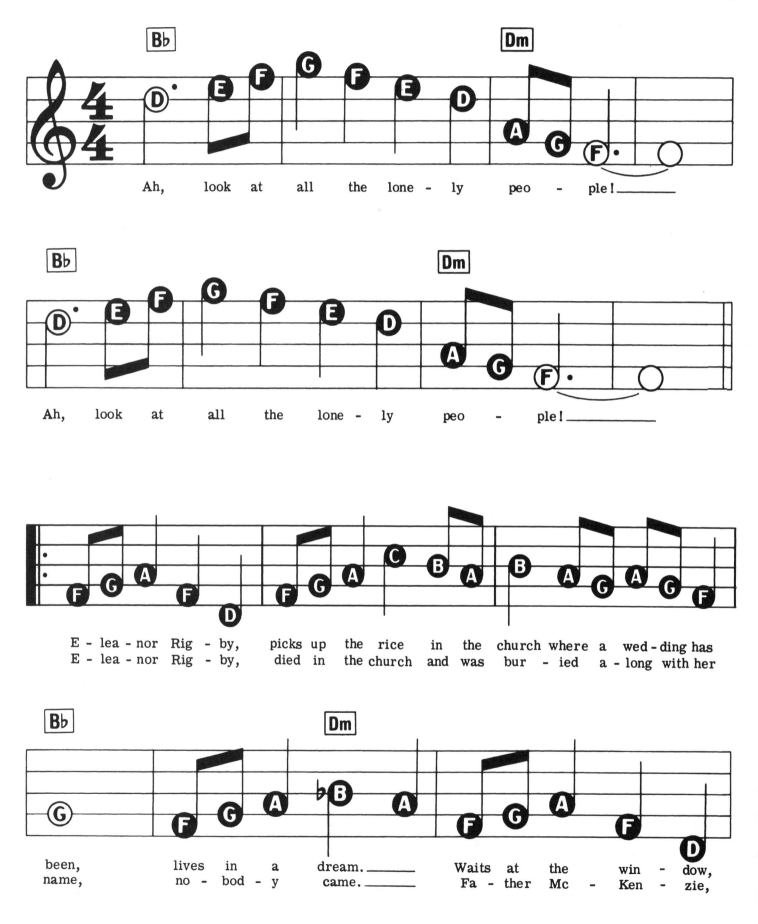

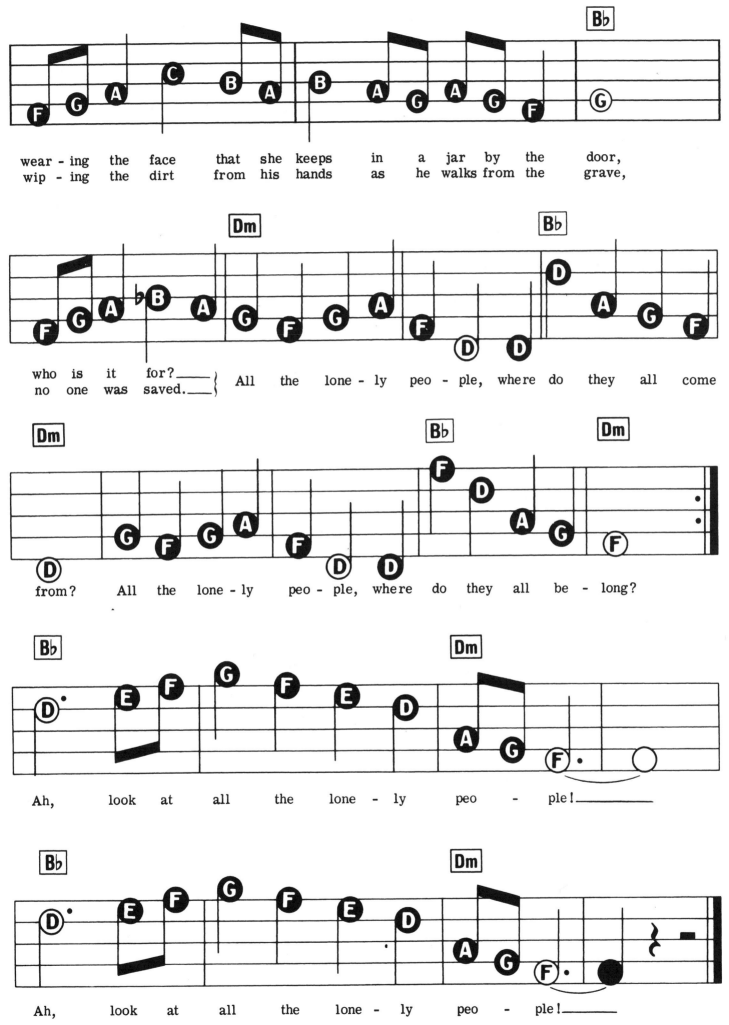

The Fool on the Hill

Registration 1
Rhythm: Rock or Bossa Nova

Words and Music by John Lennon
and Paul McCartney

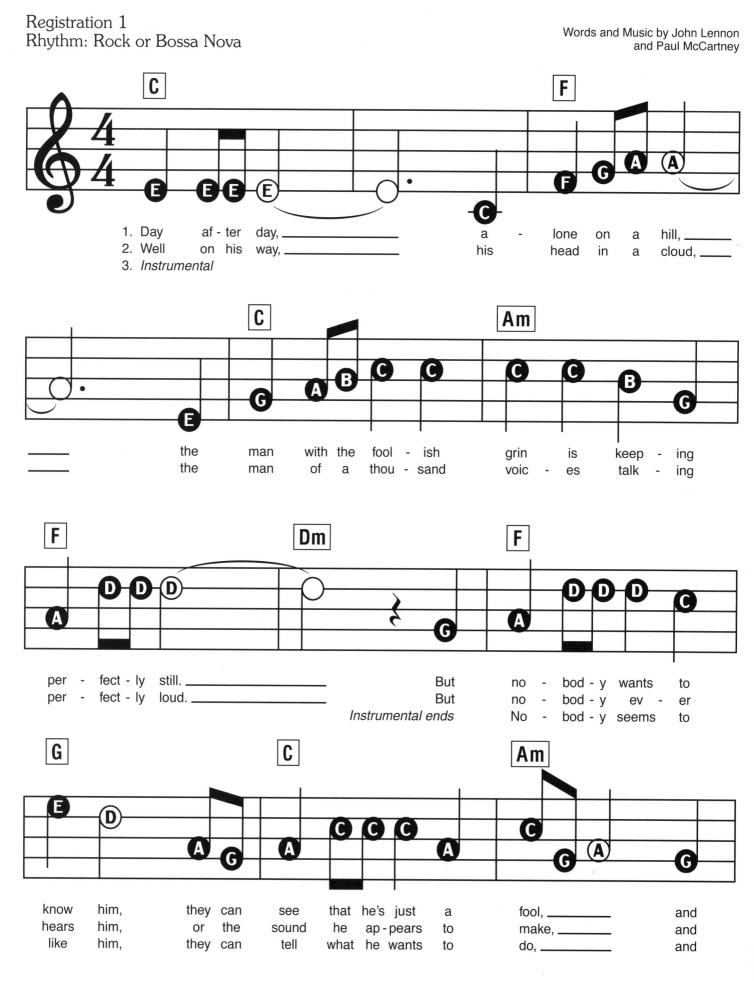

17

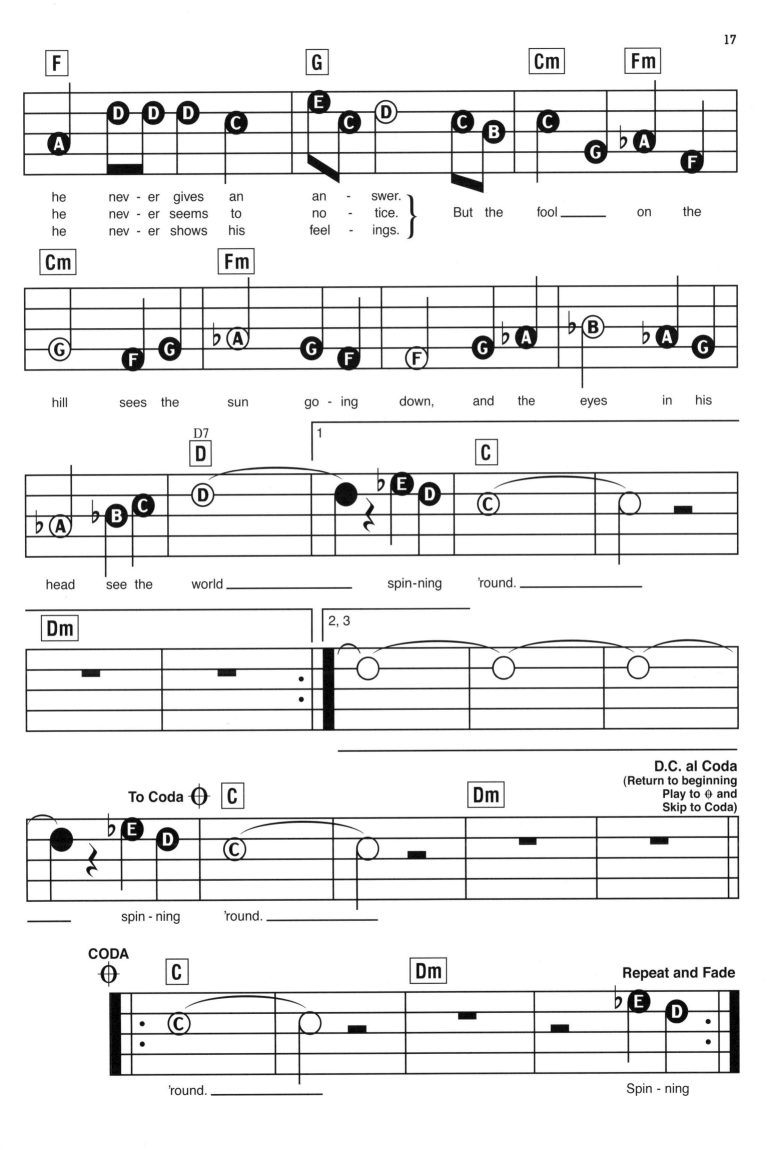

Get Back

Registration 8
Rhythm: Rock

Words and Music by John Lennon
and Paul McCartney

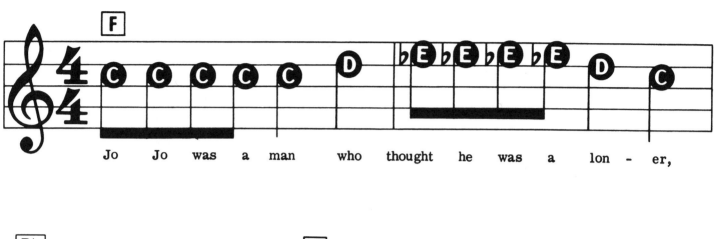

Jo Jo was a man who thought he was a lon - er,

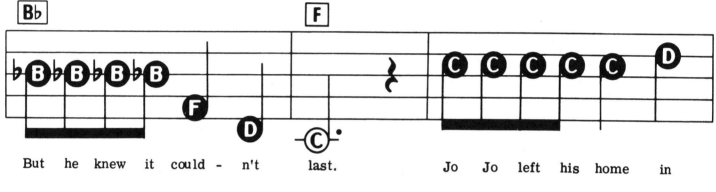

But he knew it could - n't last. Jo Jo left his home in

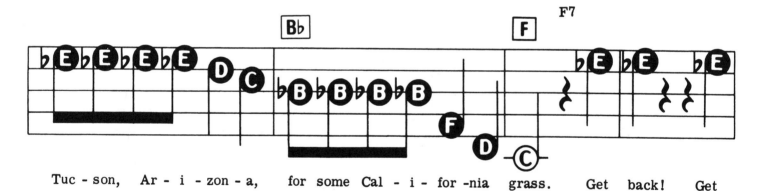

Tuc - son, Ar - i - zon - a, for some Cal - i - for - nia grass. Get back! Get

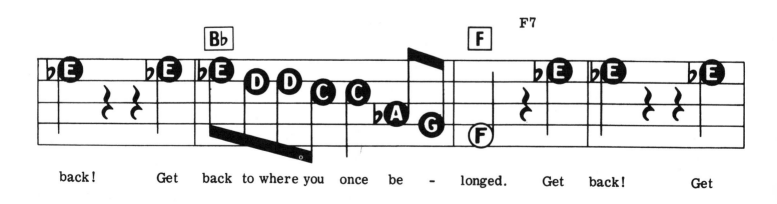

back! Get back to where you once be - longed. Get back! Get

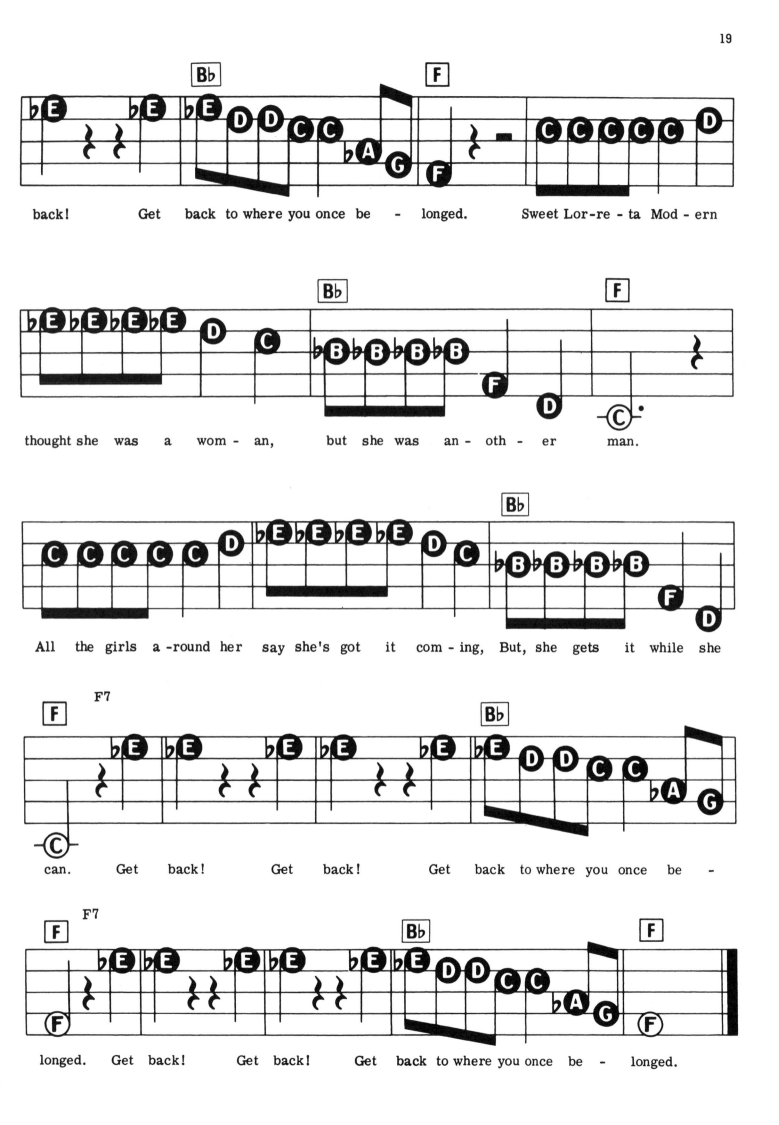

Golden Slumbers

Registration 4
Rhythm: Ballad

Words and Music by John Lennon
and Paul McCartney

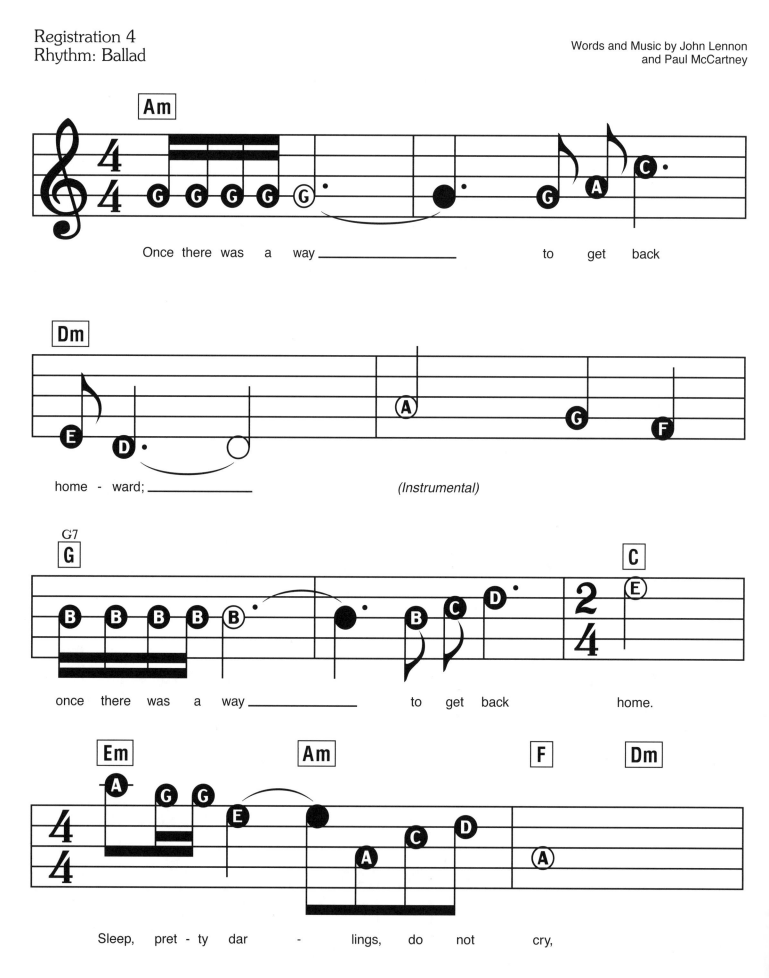

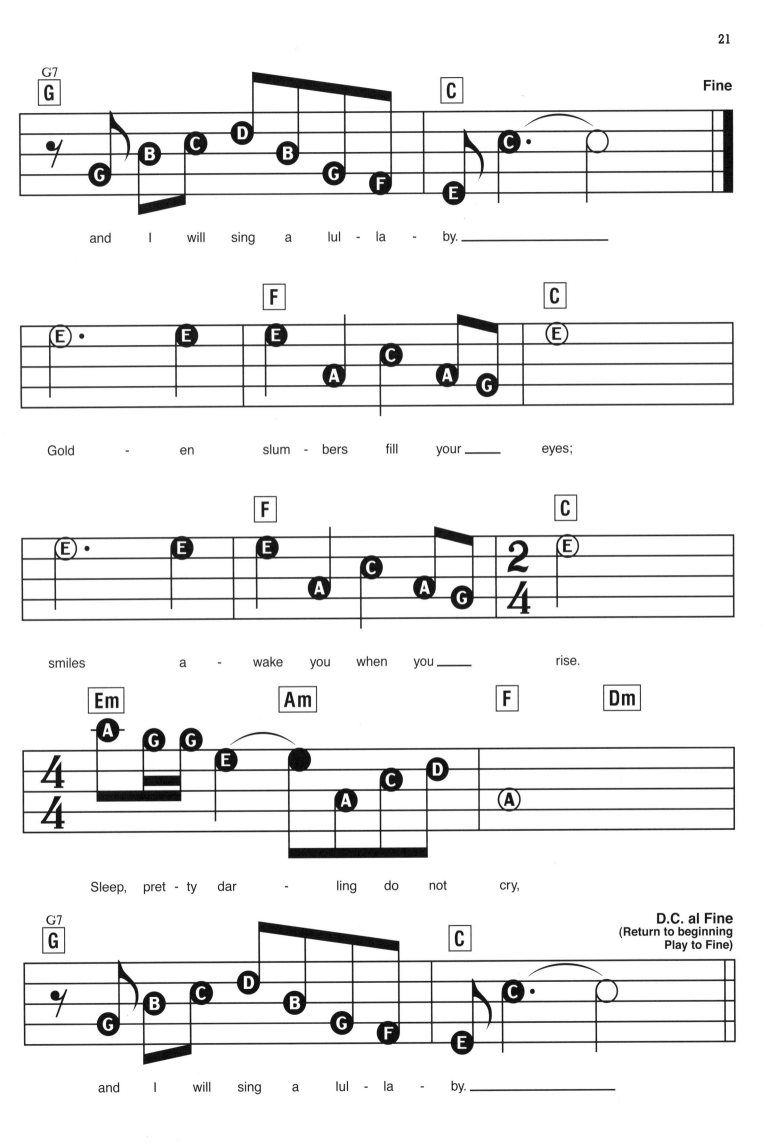

Got to Get You Into My Life

Registration 9
Rhythm: Rock or Jazz Rock

Words and Music by John Lennon
and Paul McCartney

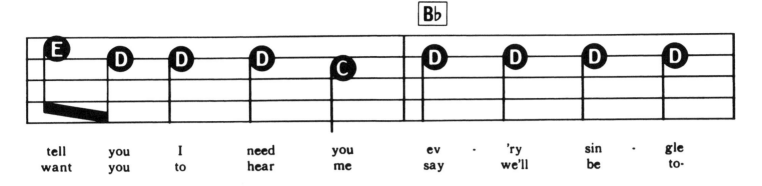

tell   you   I   need   you   ev - 'ry   sin - gle
want   you   to   hear   me   say   we'll   be   to-

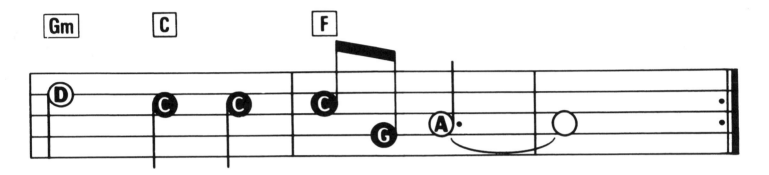

day   of   my   life?
gether   ev - 'ry   day.

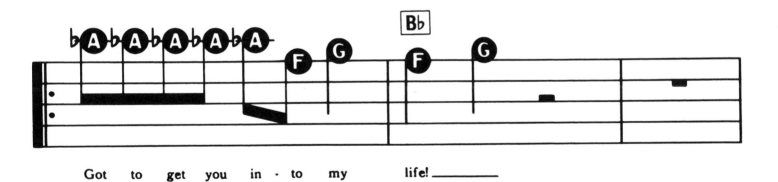

Got   to   get   you   in - to   my   life!

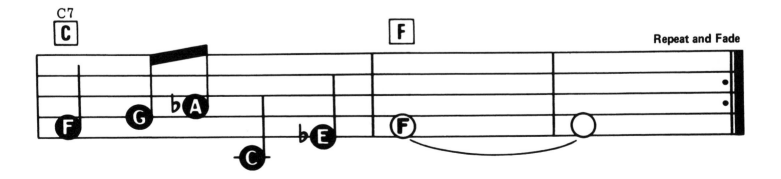

Repeat and Fade

A Hard Day's Night

Registration 7
Rhythm: Rock or Jazz Rock

Words and Music by John Lennon
and Paul McCartney

It's been a hard day's night, And I've been work - ing like a
work all day To get you mon - ey to buy

dog._____ It's been a hard day's night, I should be
things,_____ And it's_____ worth it just to hear you say You're gon - na

sleep - ing like a log._____ But when I get home to you, I find the
give me ev - 'ry - thing._____ So why I love to come home, Cos when I

things that you do will made me feel_____ al - right. You know I
get you a - lone you know I'll be_____ o -

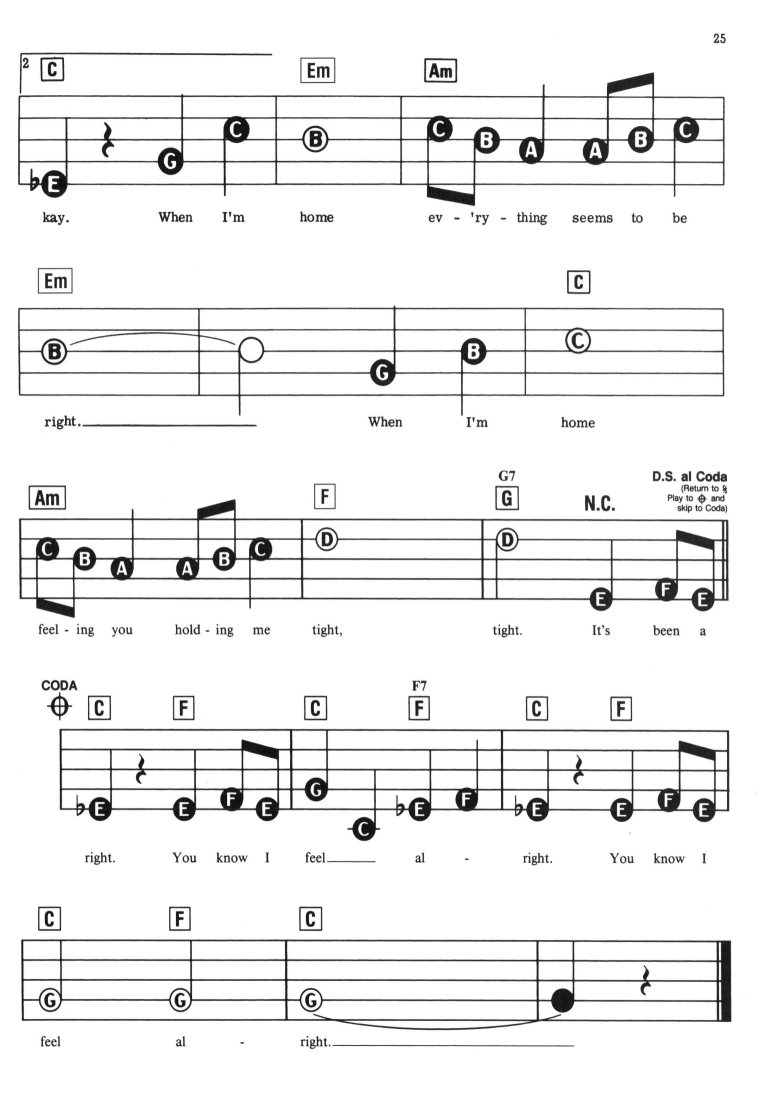

Hello, Goodbye

Registration 3
Rhythm: Rock or Latin Rock

Words and Music by John Lennon
and Paul McCartney

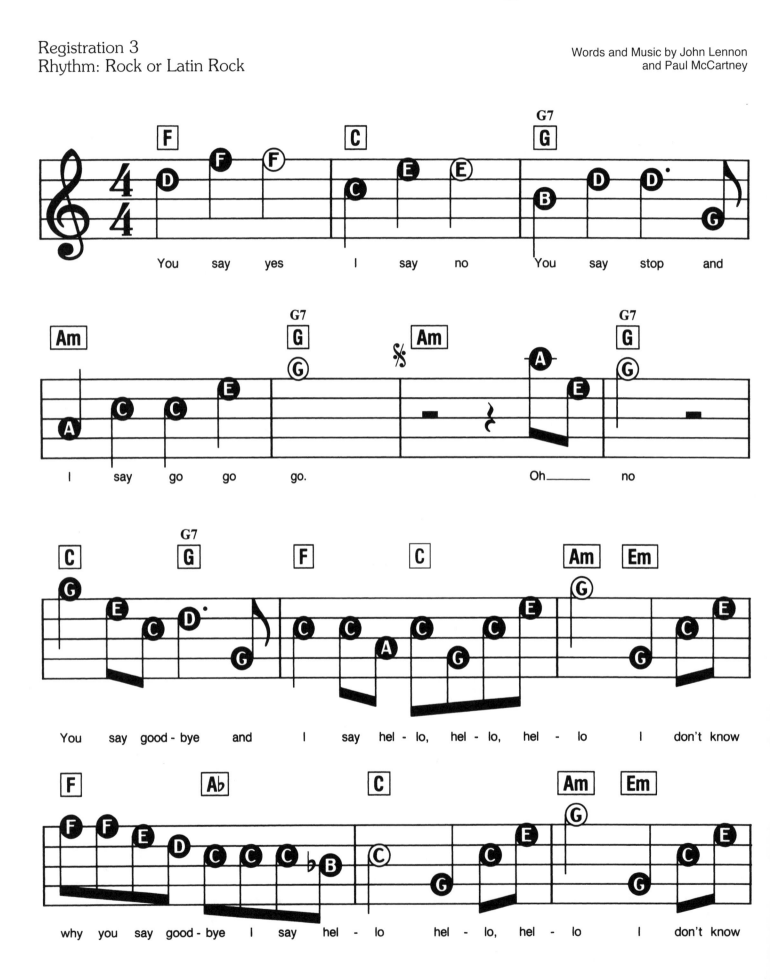

27

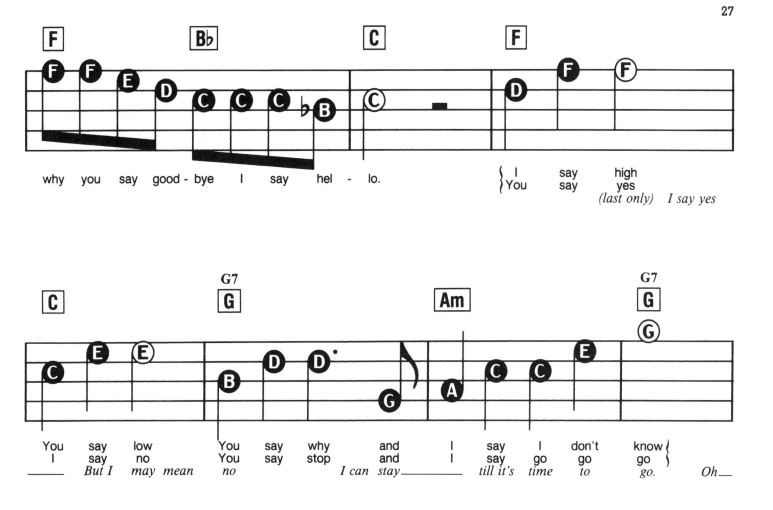

why you say good-bye I say hel-lo.

{ I say high
You say yes
(last only) I say yes

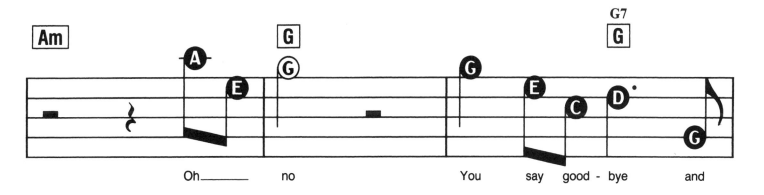

You say low ___ You say why and I say I don't know }
I say no / But I may mean no / You say why stop and I say go go go ___ Oh___
You say why and I can stay ___ till it's time to go. go.

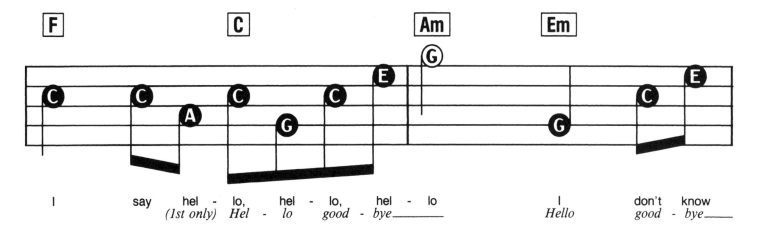

Oh___ no   You say good-bye and

I say hel-lo, hel-lo, hel-lo   I don't know
(1st only) Hel-lo good-bye___   Hello good-bye___

28

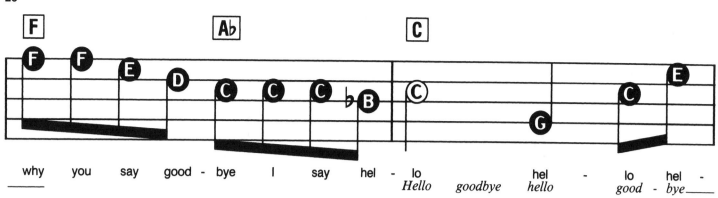

why you say good - bye I say hel - lo *Hello goodbye hello - lo hel - good - bye*

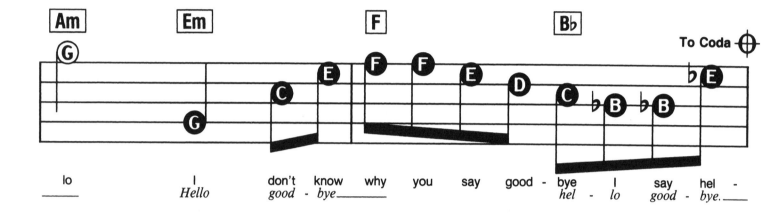

lo *Hello* don't know why you say good - bye I say hel - *good - bye* *hel - lo say good - bye.*

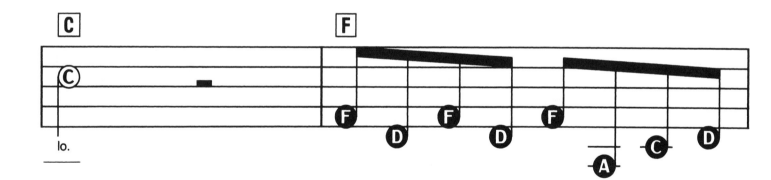

lo.

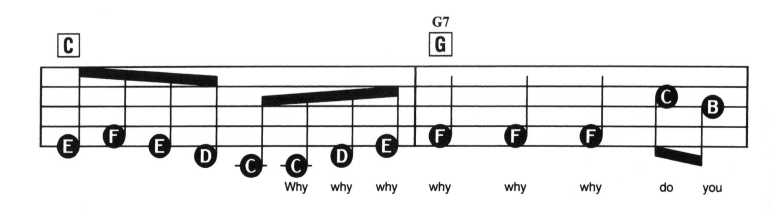

Why why why why why why do you

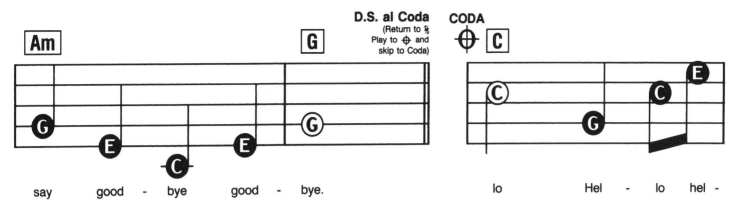

D.S. al Coda
(Return to %
Play to ⊕ and
skip to Coda)

CODA

say good - bye good - bye.

lo   Hel - lo   hel -

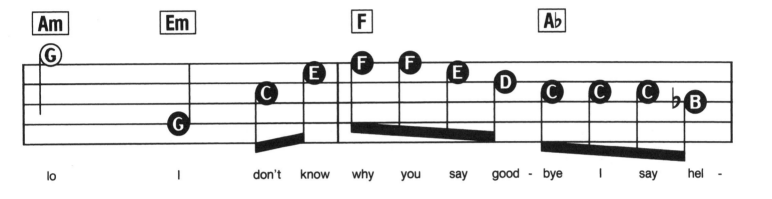

lo   I   don't know why you say good - bye   I   say hel -

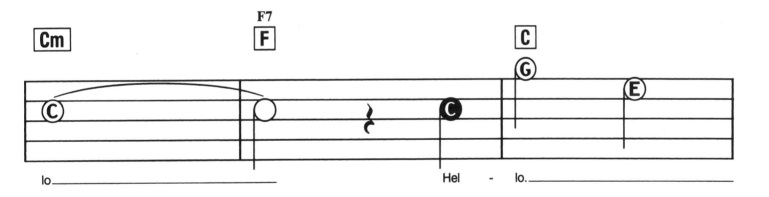

lo_____   Hel - lo._____

Repeat and Fade

_____   He - la   he - ba_____   hel - lo - a.

Help!

Registration 3
Rhythm: Rock or Jazz Rock

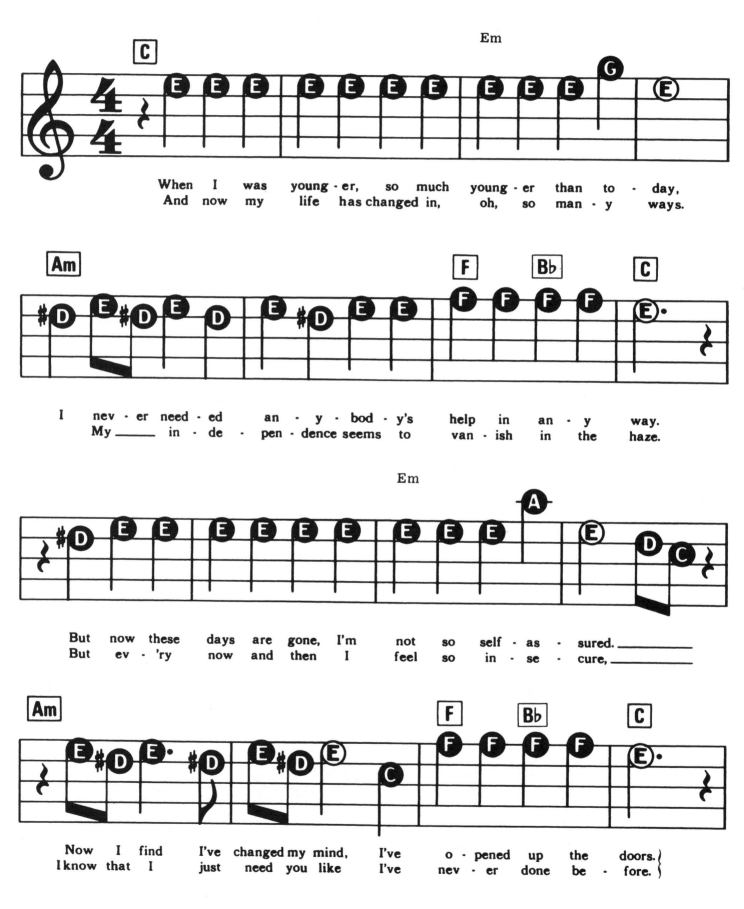

Words and Music by John Lennon
and Paul McCartney

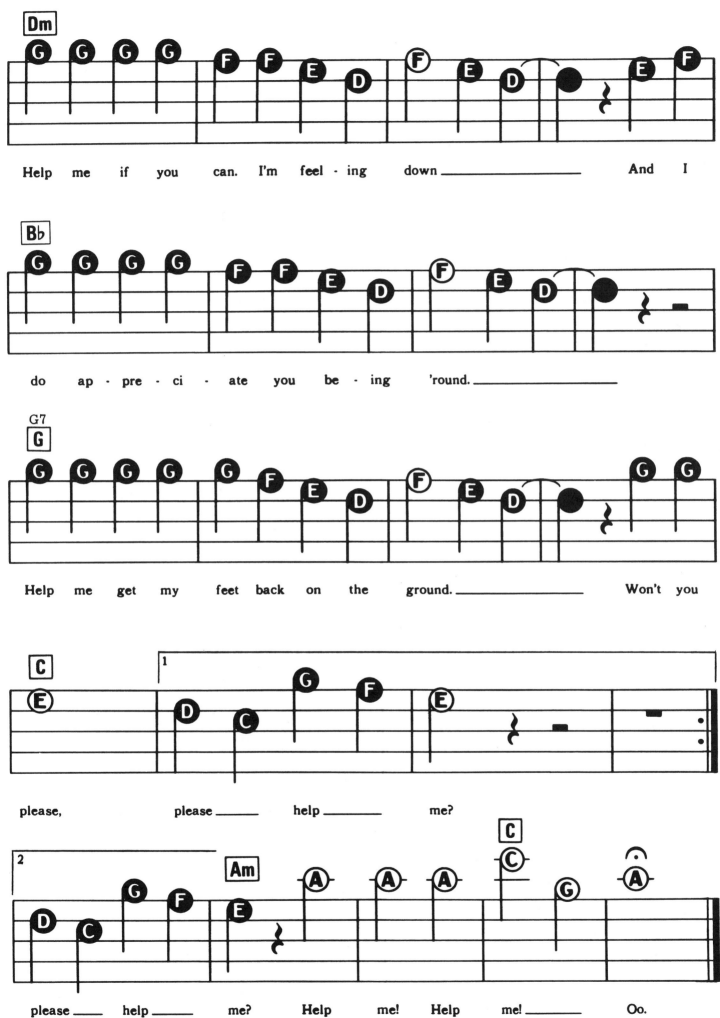

Helter Skelter

Registration 4
Rhythm: Rock

Words and Music by John Lennon
and Paul McCartney

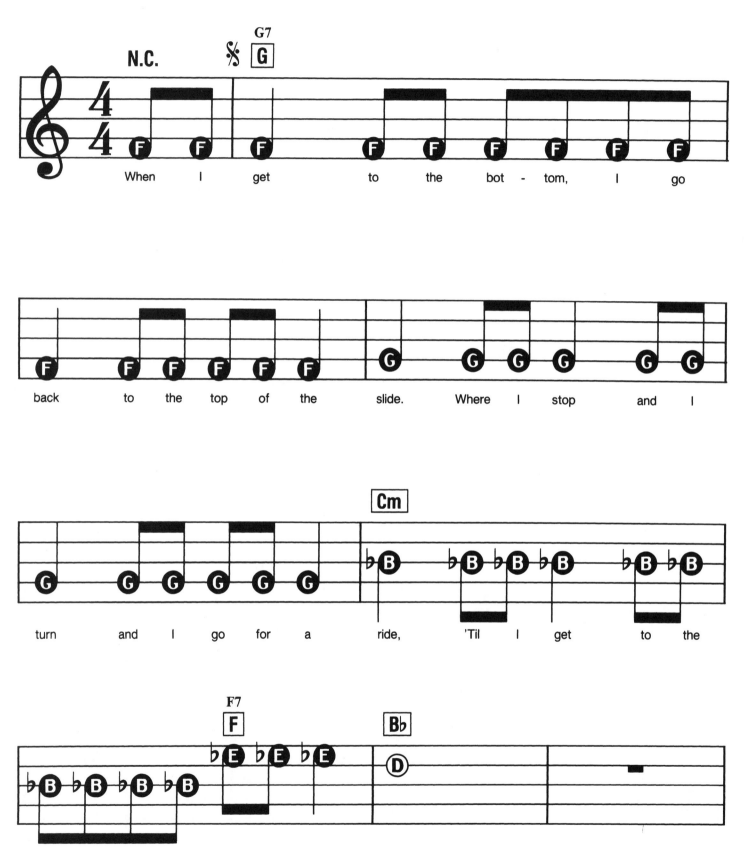

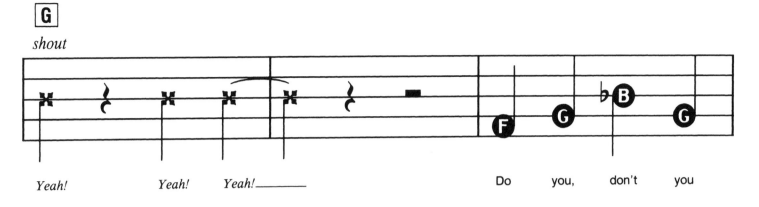

Yeah!   Yeah!   Yeah!_____   Do   you,   don't   you

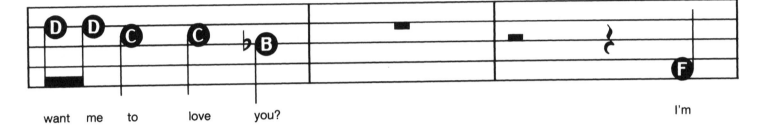

want   me   to   love   you?   I'm

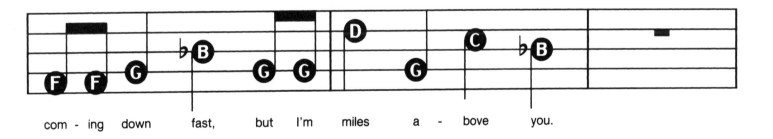

com - ing   down   fast,   but   I'm   miles   a - bove   you.

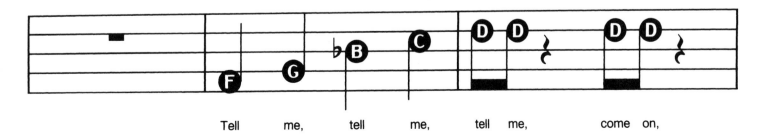

Tell   me,   tell   me,   tell   me,   come   on,

34

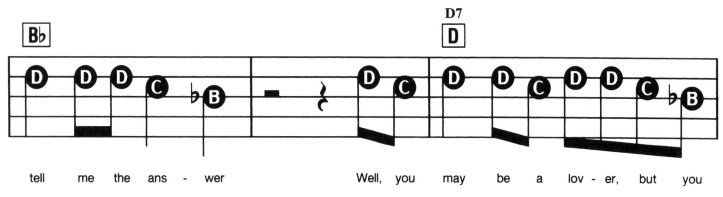

tell me the ans - wer   Well, you may be a lov - er, but you

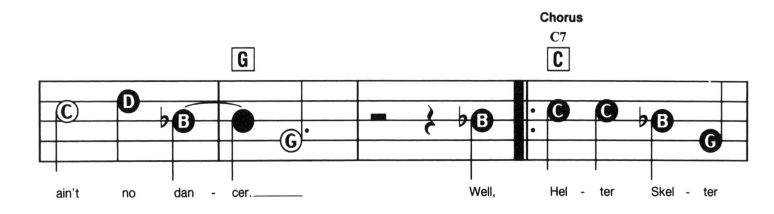

ain't no dan - cer._____   Well,   Hel - ter Skel - ter

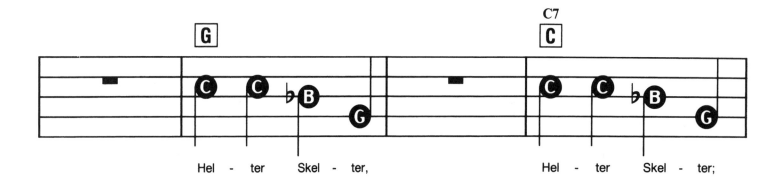

Hel - ter Skel - ter,   Hel - ter Skel - ter;

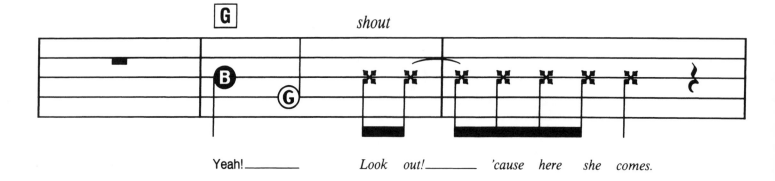

Yeah!_____   *Look out!*_____ *'cause here she comes.*

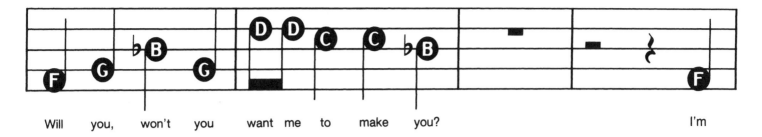

Will you, won't you want me to make you? I'm

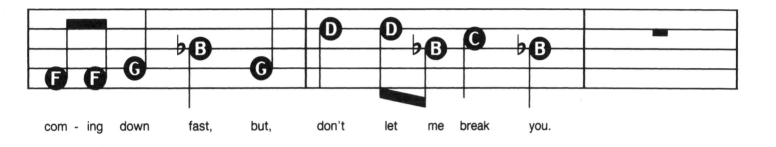

com - ing down fast, but, don't let me break you.

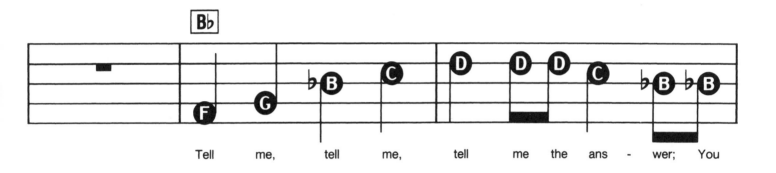

Tell me, tell me, tell me the ans - wer; You

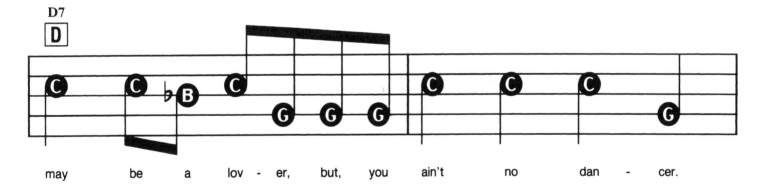

may be a lov - er, but, you ain't no dan - cer.

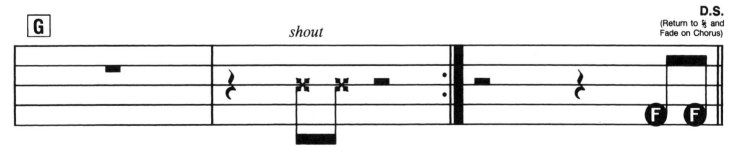

Look out! When I

Hey Jude

Registration 2
Rhythm: Pops or 8-Beat

Words and Music by John Lennon
and Paul McCartney

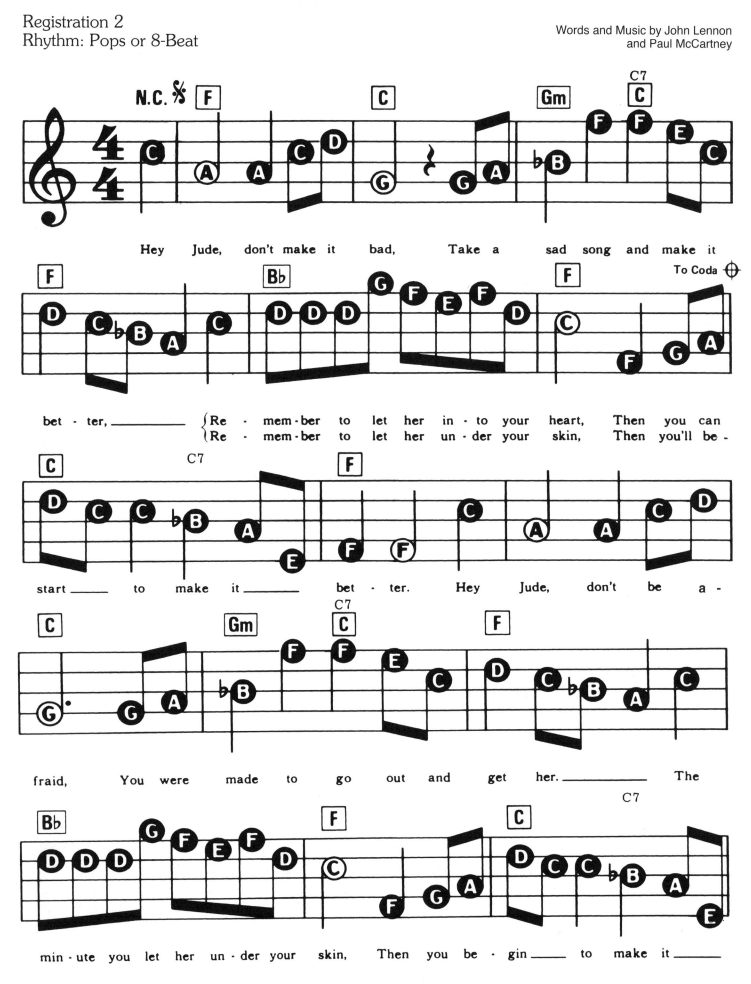

I Am the Walrus

Registration 5
Rhythm: Rock

Words and Music by John Lennon
and Paul McCartney

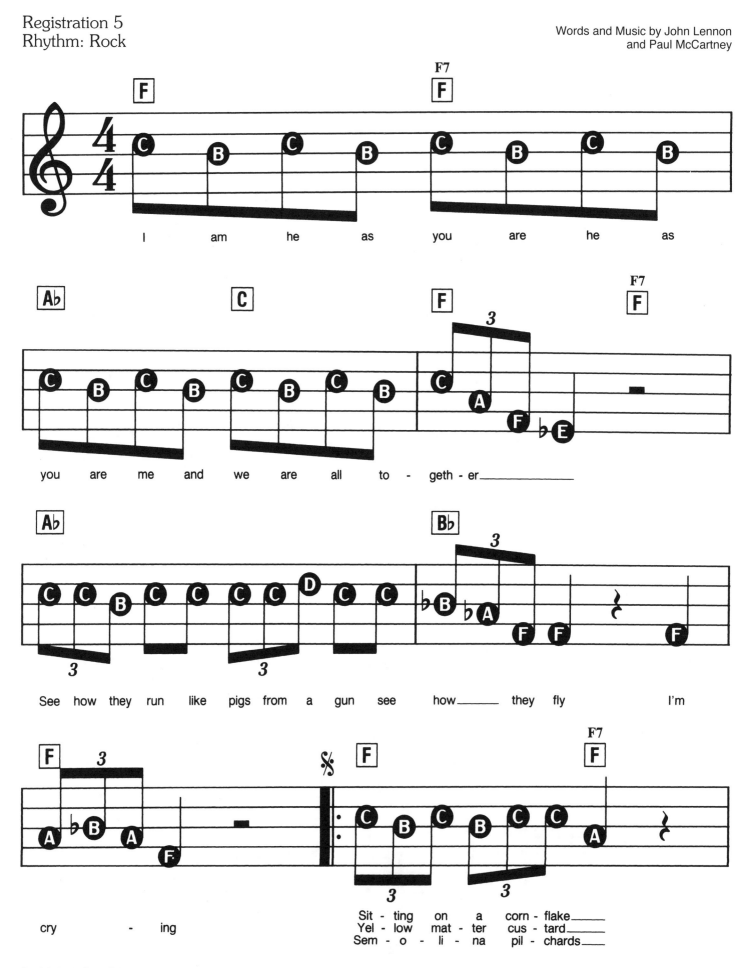

39

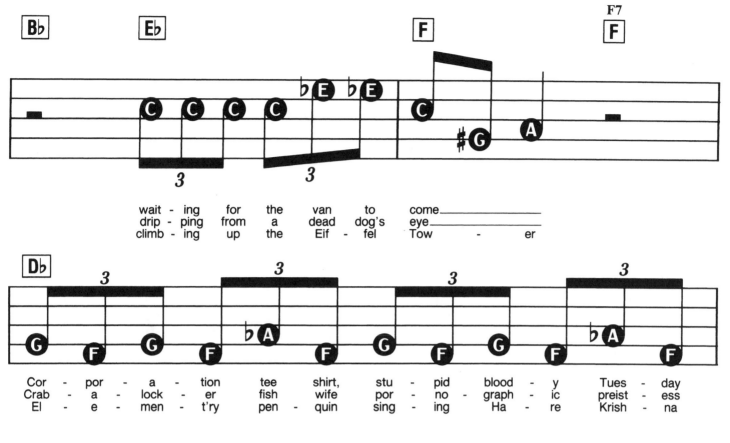

waiting for the van to come___
drip - ping from a dead dog's eye___
climb - ing up the Eif - fel Tow - er

Cor - por - a - tion tee shirt, stu - pid blood - y Tues - day
Crab - a - lock - er fish wife por - no - graph - ic preist - ess
El - e - men - t'ry pen - quin sing - ing Ha - re Krish - na

man you been a naugh - ty boy you let your face grow
boy you been a naugh - ty girl you let your knick - ers
man you should have seen them kick - ing Ed - gar Al - lan

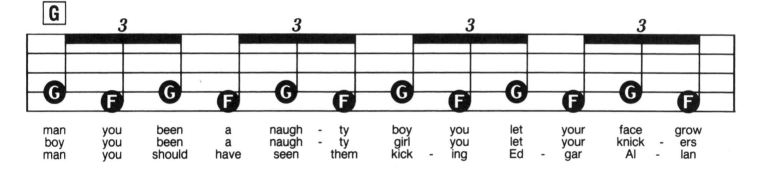

long.
down.
Poe.

I am the egg man Oh they are the

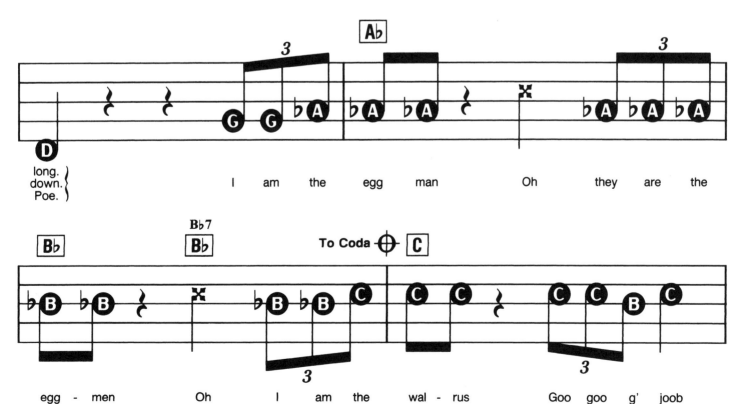

egg - men Oh I am the wal - rus Goo goo g' joob

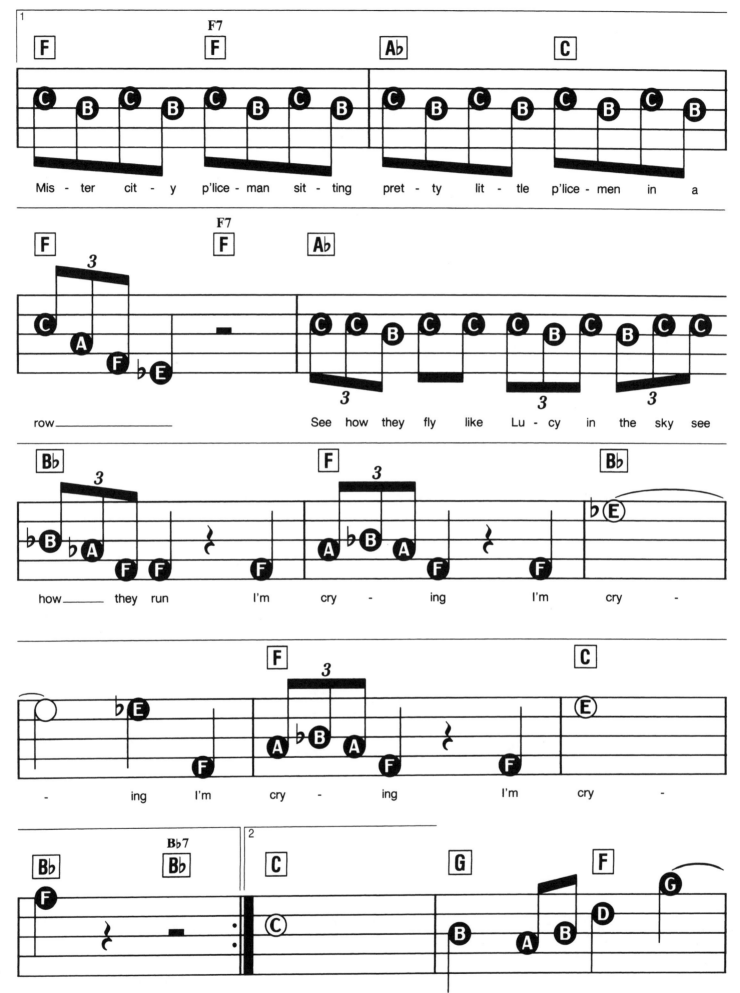

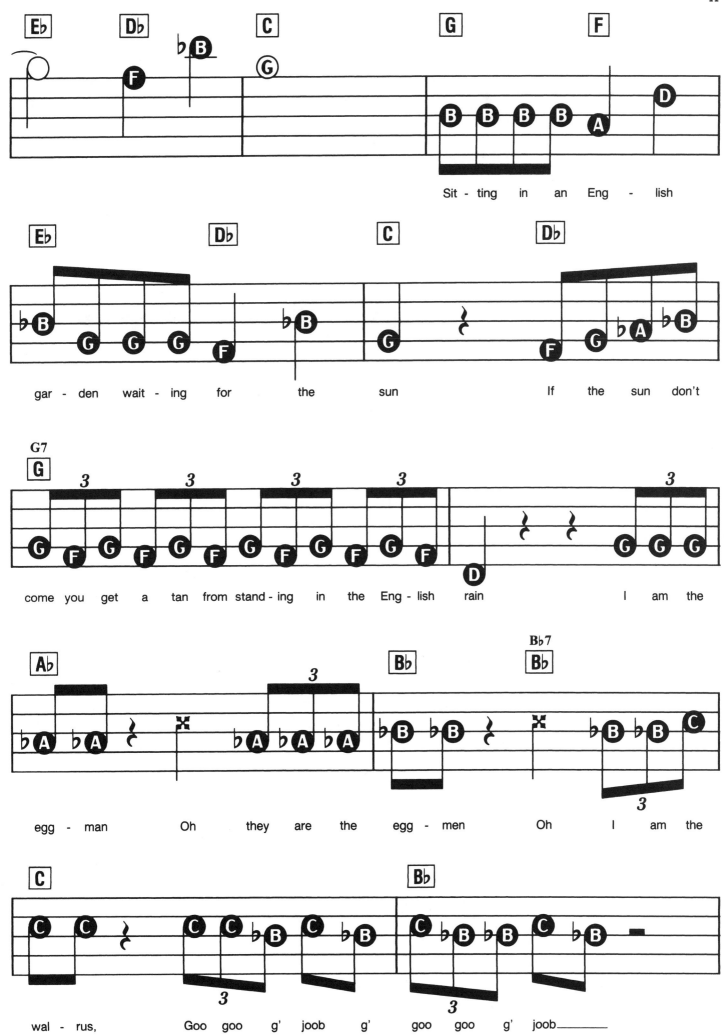

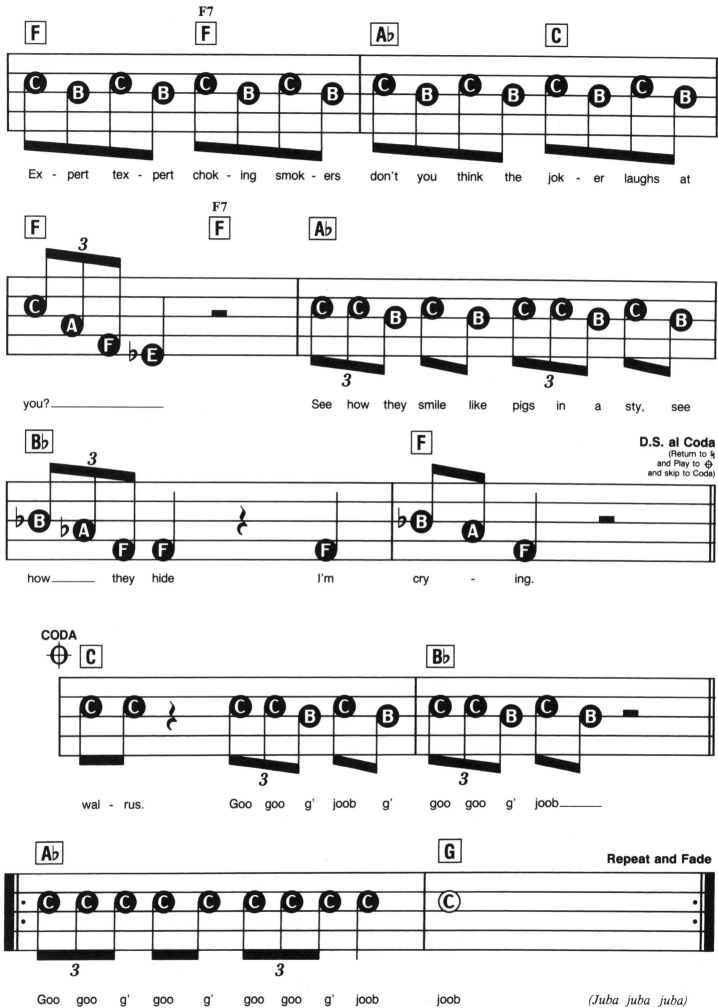

42

Ex - pert tex - pert chok - ing smok - ers don't you think the jok - er laughs at

you?_____ See how they smile like pigs in a sty, see

how____ they hide I'm cry - ing.

wal - rus. Goo goo g' joob g' goo goo g' joob____

Goo goo g' goo g' goo goo g' joob joob *(Juba juba juba)*

D.S. al Coda
(Return to ☩
and Play to ⊕
and skip to Coda)

CODA

Repeat and Fade

Norwegian Wood
(This Bird Has Flown)

Registration 4
Rhythm: Waltz

Words and Music by John Lennon
and Paul McCartney

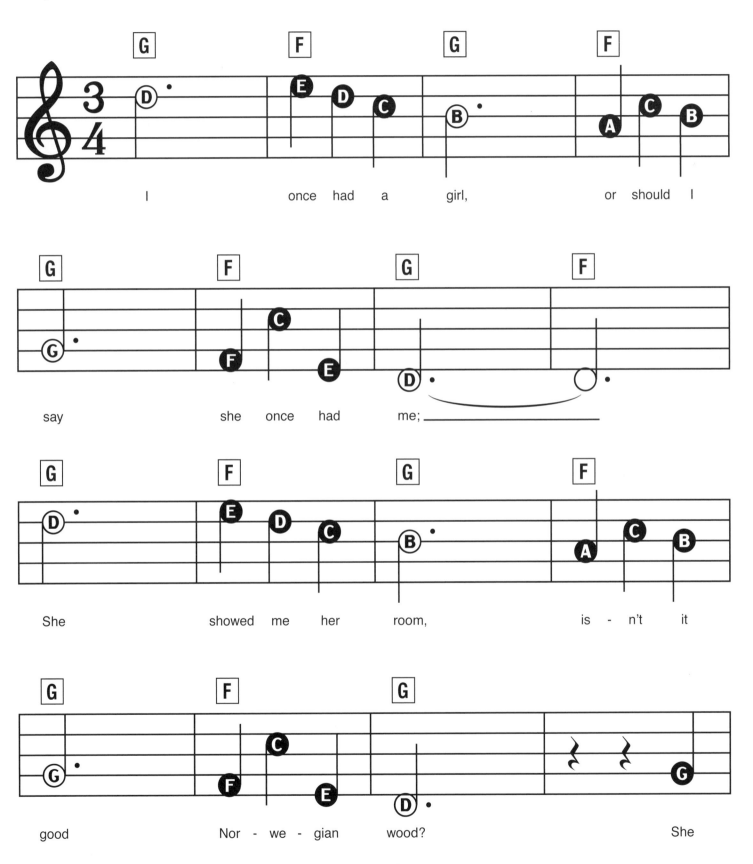

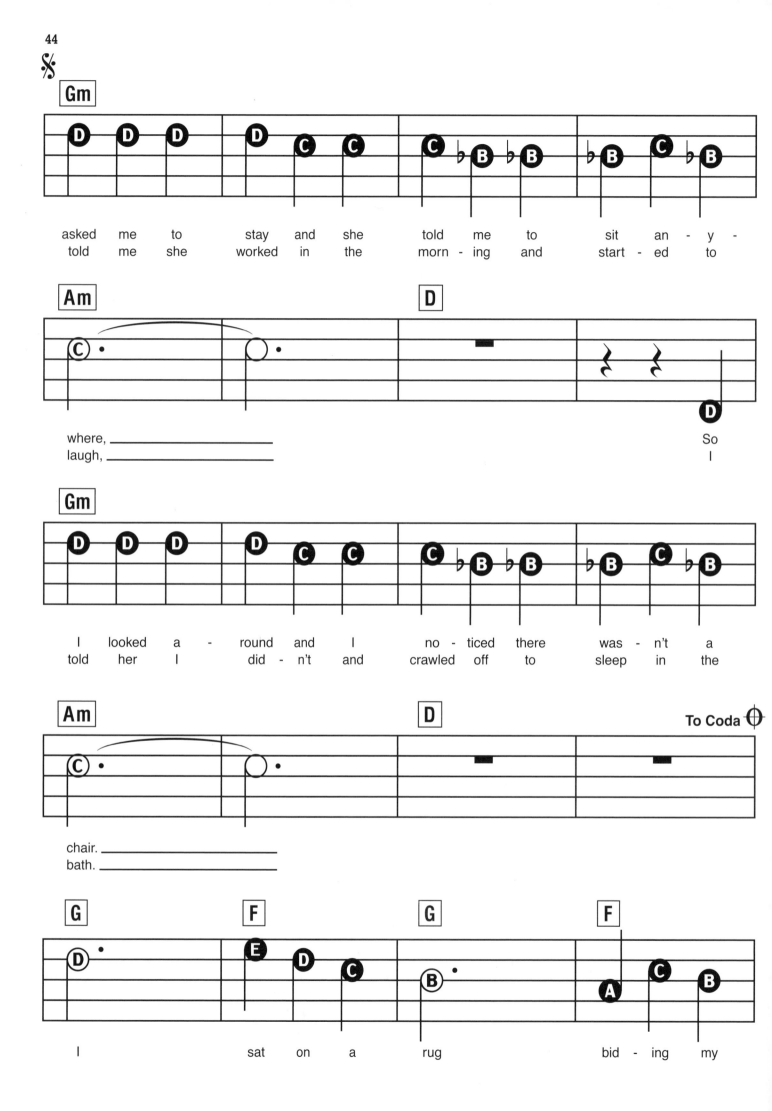

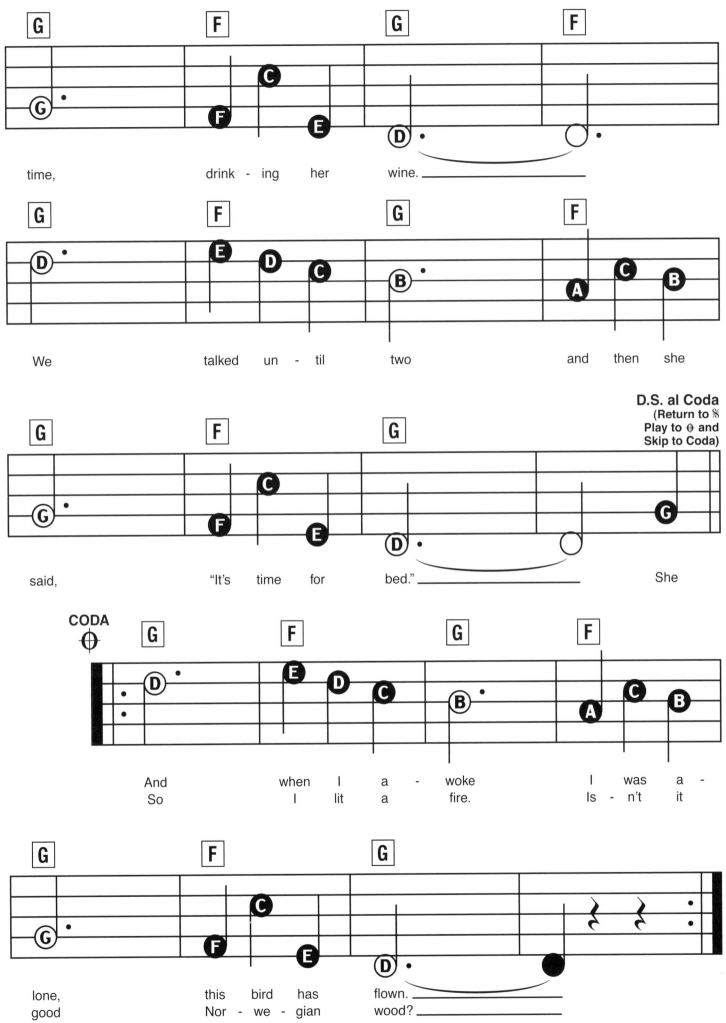

I Want to Hold Your Hand

Registration 3
Rhythm: Rock

Words and Music by John Lennon
and Paul McCartney

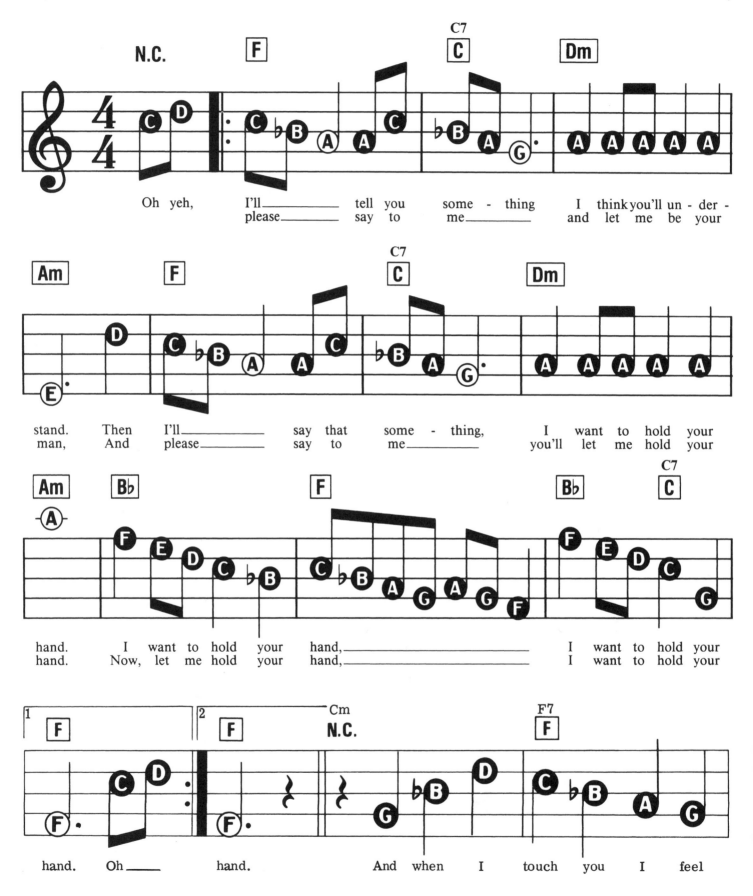

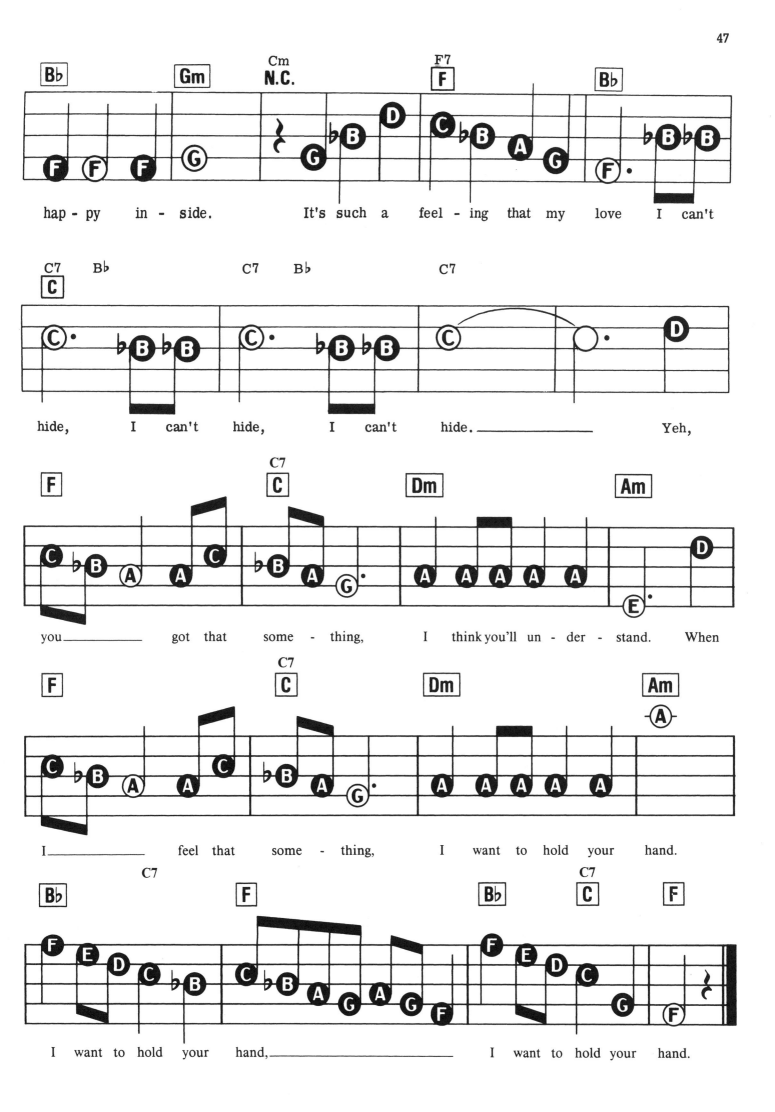

I'll Follow the Sun

Registration 9
Rhythm: Rock or Latin

Words and Music by John Lennon
and Paul McCartney

One — day you'll look to see I've
Some — day you'll know I was the

gone, For to - mor - row may rain, so I'll fol - low the
one, But to - mor - row may rain, so I'll fol - low the

sun. _____ sun.

And now the time has come and

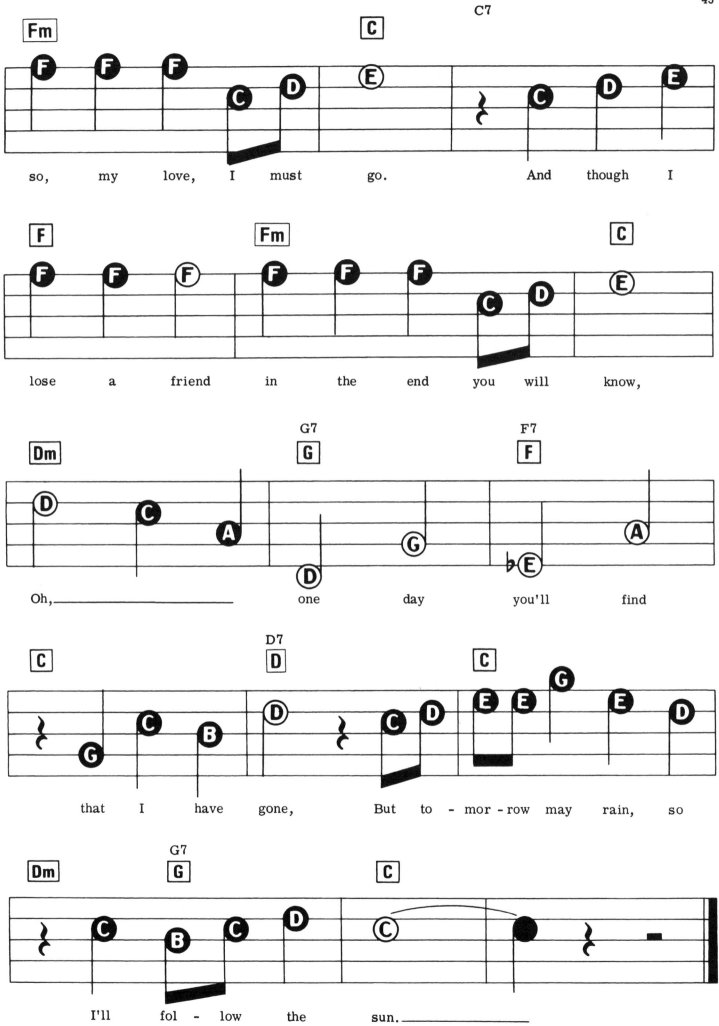

Lady Madonna

Registration 4
Rhythm: Rock

Words and Music by John Lennon
and Paul McCartney

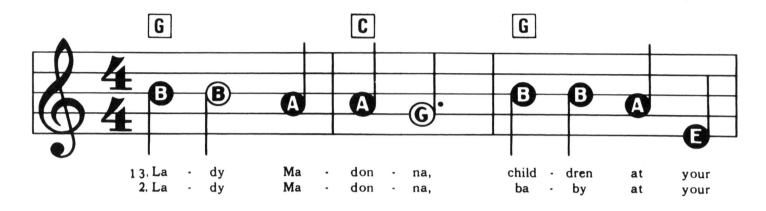

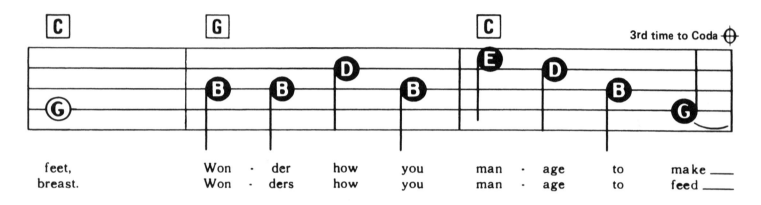

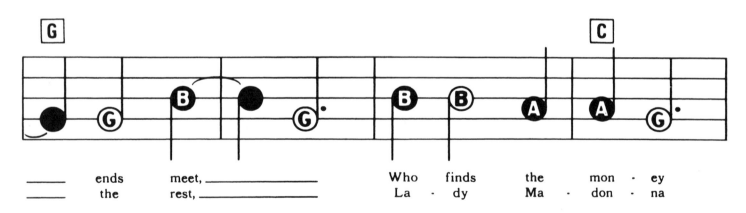

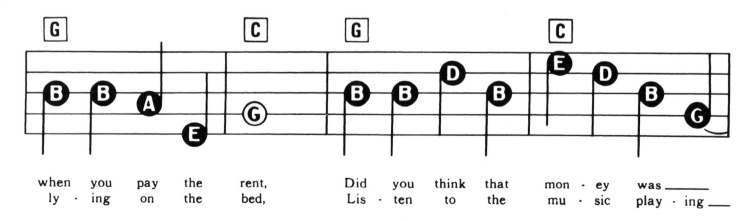

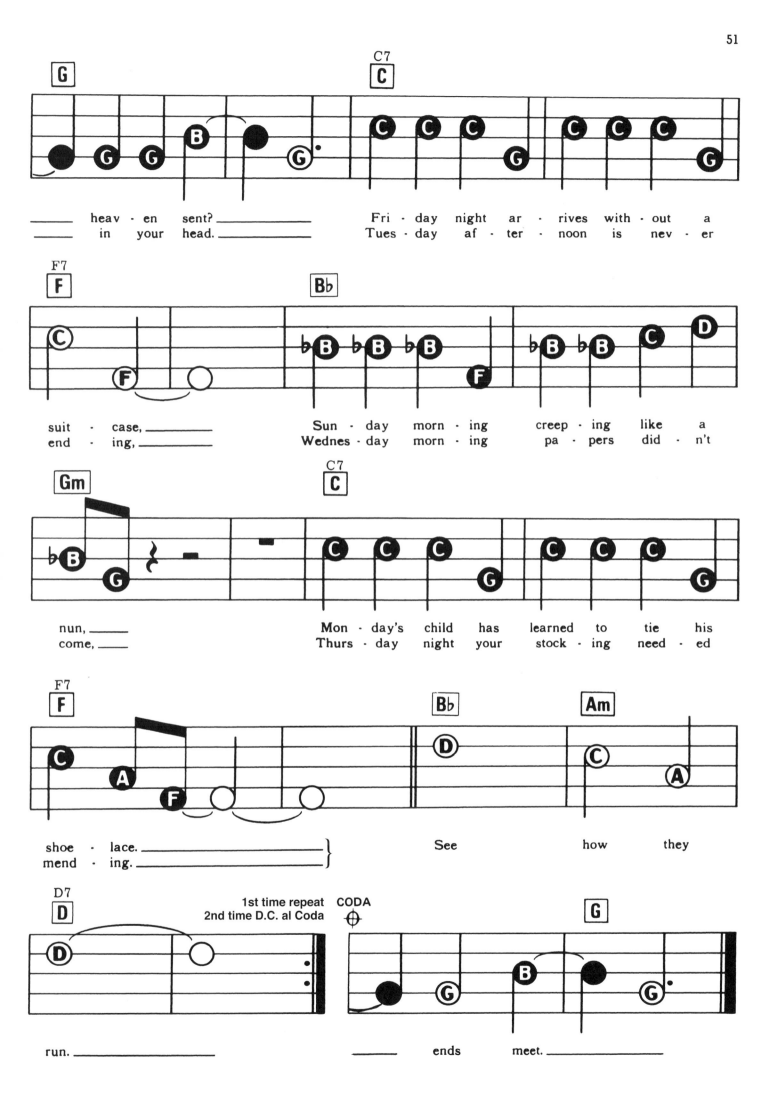

Let It Be

Registration 3
Rhythm: Rock

Words and Music by John Lennon
and Paul McCartney

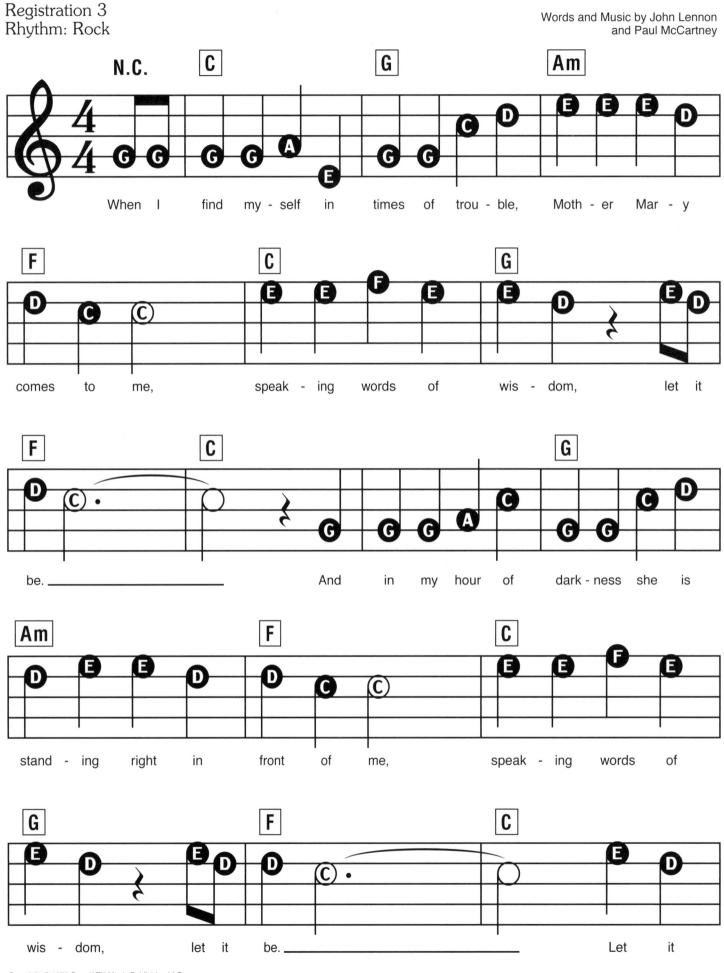

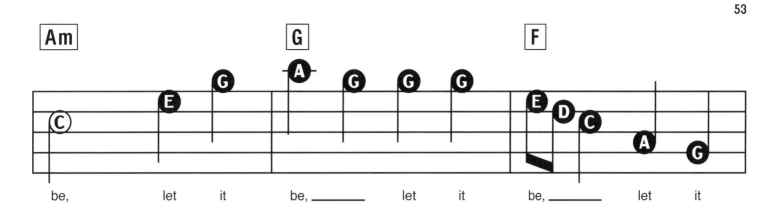

be,   let it   be, _____ let it   be, _____ let it

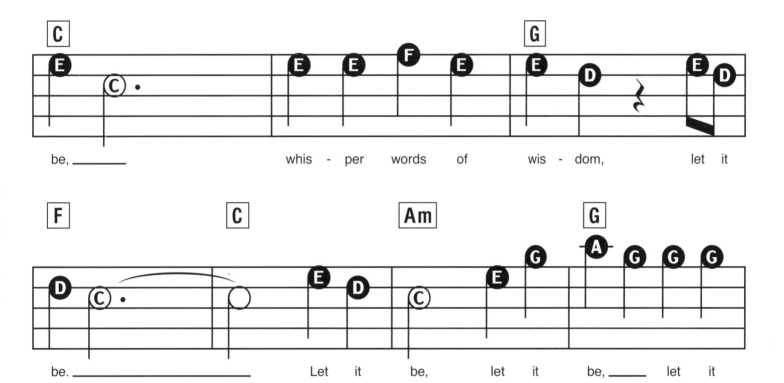

be, _____   whis - per words of   wis - dom,   let it

be. _____ Let it be,   let it   be, _____ let it

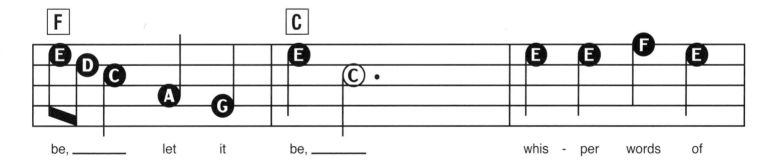

be, _____ let it   be, _____   whis - per words of

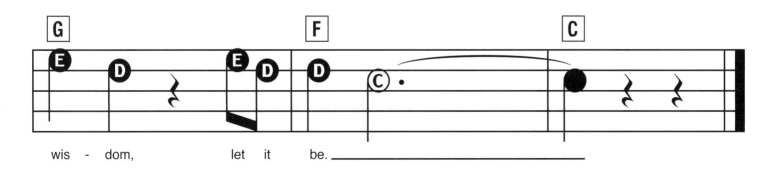

wis - dom,   let it   be. _____

Love Me Do

Registration 4
Rhythm: Rock

Words and Music by John Lennon
and Paul McCartney

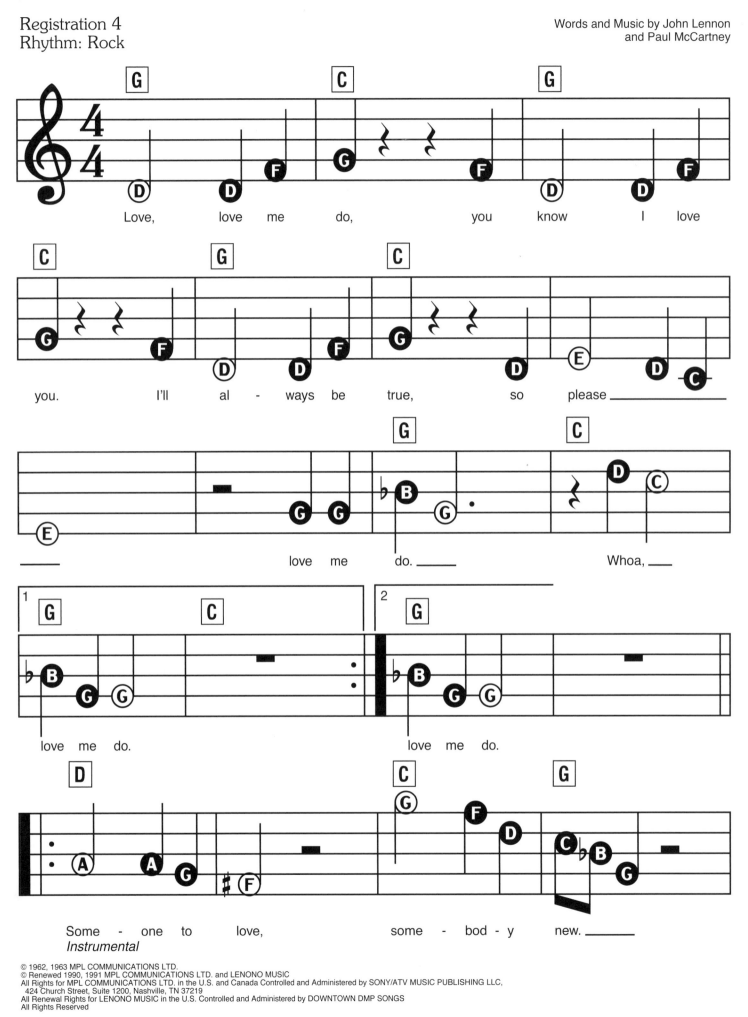

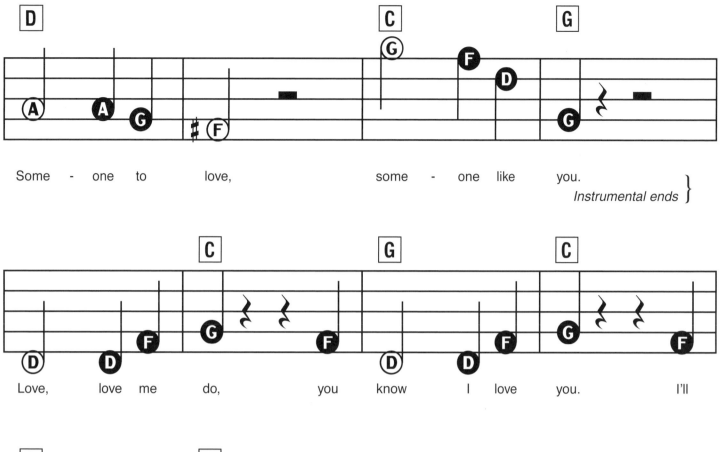

Some - one to love, some - one like you.
Instrumental ends }

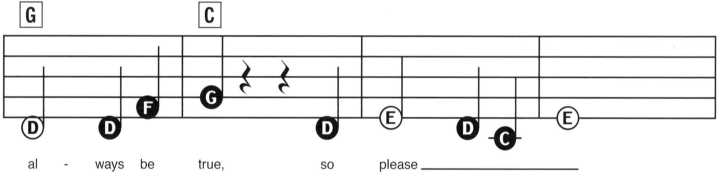

Love, love me do, you know I love you. I'll

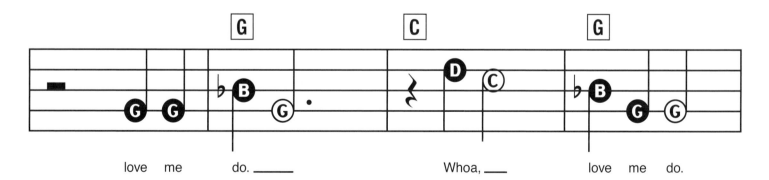

al - ways be true, so please ____

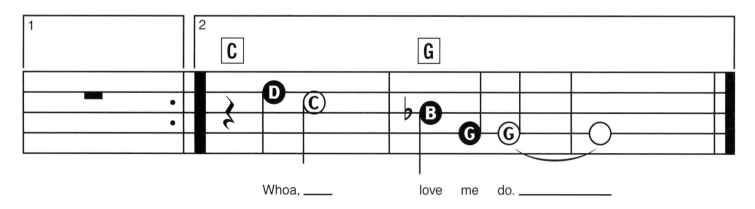

love me do. ____ Whoa, ____ love me do.

Whoa, ____ love me do. ____

Lucy in the Sky with Diamonds

Registration 8
Rhythm: Waltz

Words and Music by John Lennon
and Paul McCartney

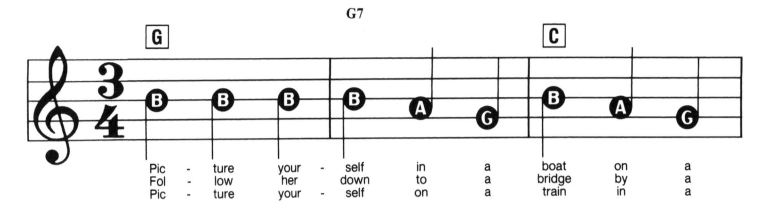

Pic - ture your - self in a boat on a
Fol - low her down to a bridge by a
Pic - ture your - self on a train in a

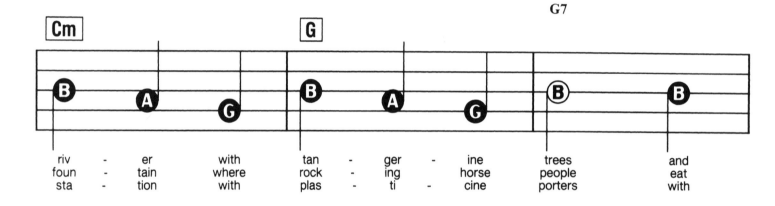

riv - er with tan - ger - ine trees and
foun - tain where tan rock - ing horse people eat
sta - tion with plas - ti - cine porters with

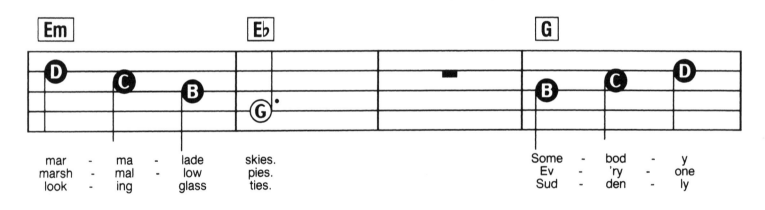

mar - ma - lade skies. Some - bod - y
marsh - mal - low pies. Ev - 'ry - one
look - ing glass ties. Sud - den - ly

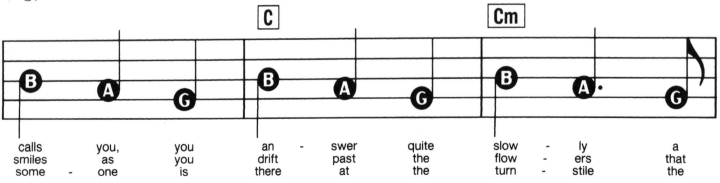

calls you, you an - swer quite slow - ly a
smiles as you drift past the flow - ers that
some - one is there at the turn - stile the

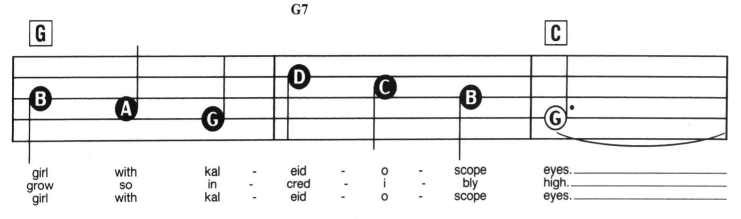

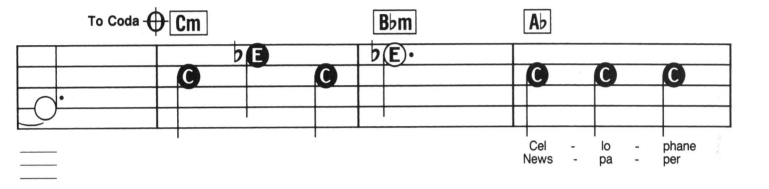

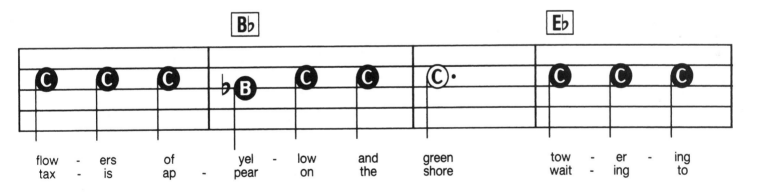

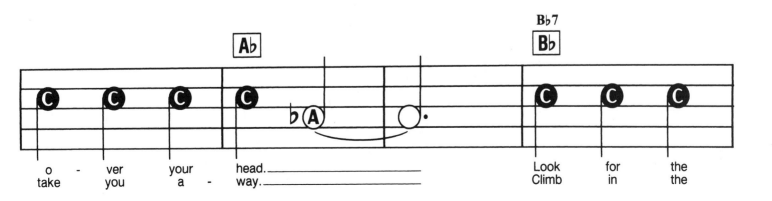

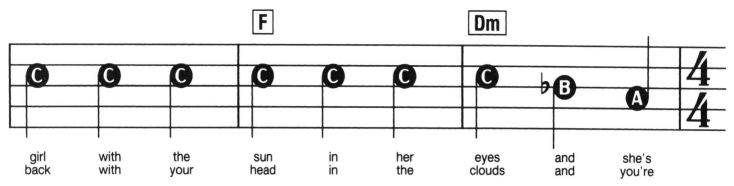

girl with the sun in her eyes and she's
back with your head in the clouds and you're

Rhythm: Rock

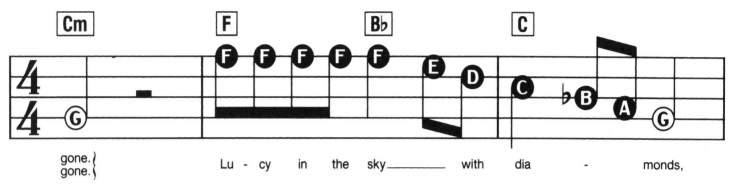

gone.
gone.   Lu - cy in the sky_____ with dia - monds,

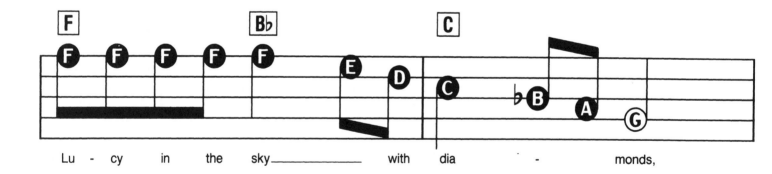

Lu - cy in the sky_____ with dia - monds,

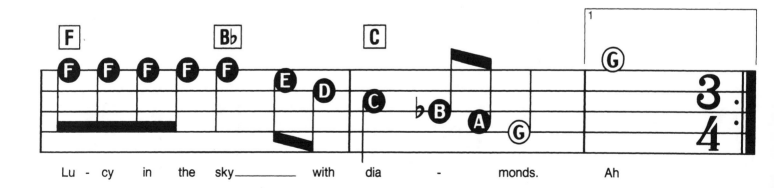

Lu - cy in the sky_____ with dia - monds.   Ah

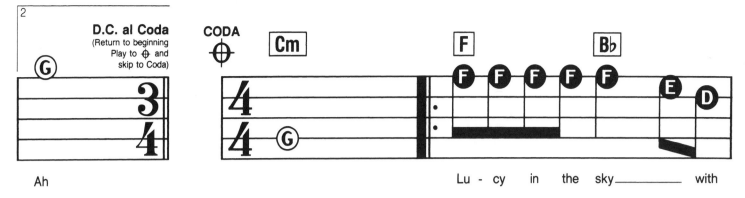

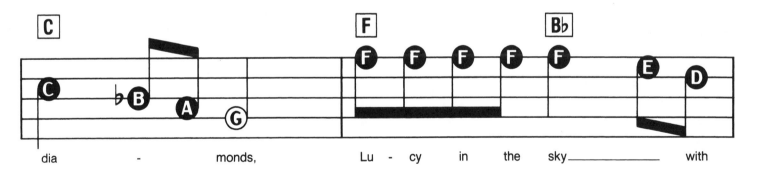

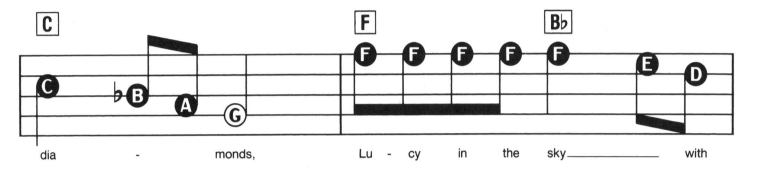

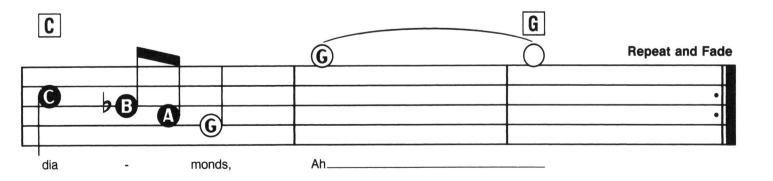

Michelle

Registration 1
Rhythm: Rock

Words and Music by John Lennon
and Paul McCartney

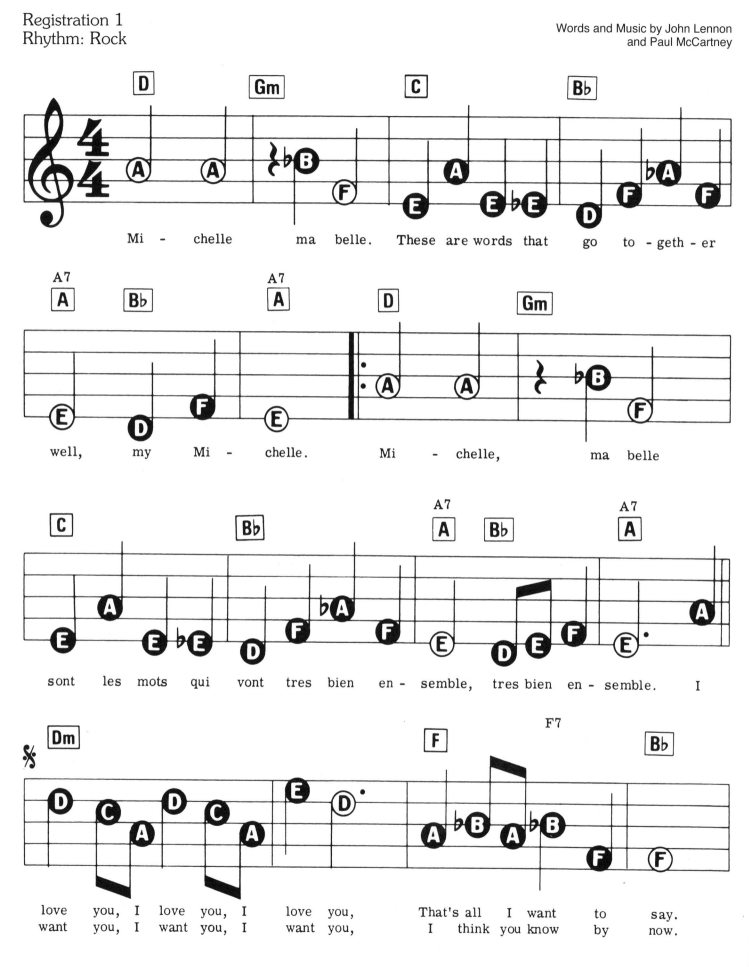

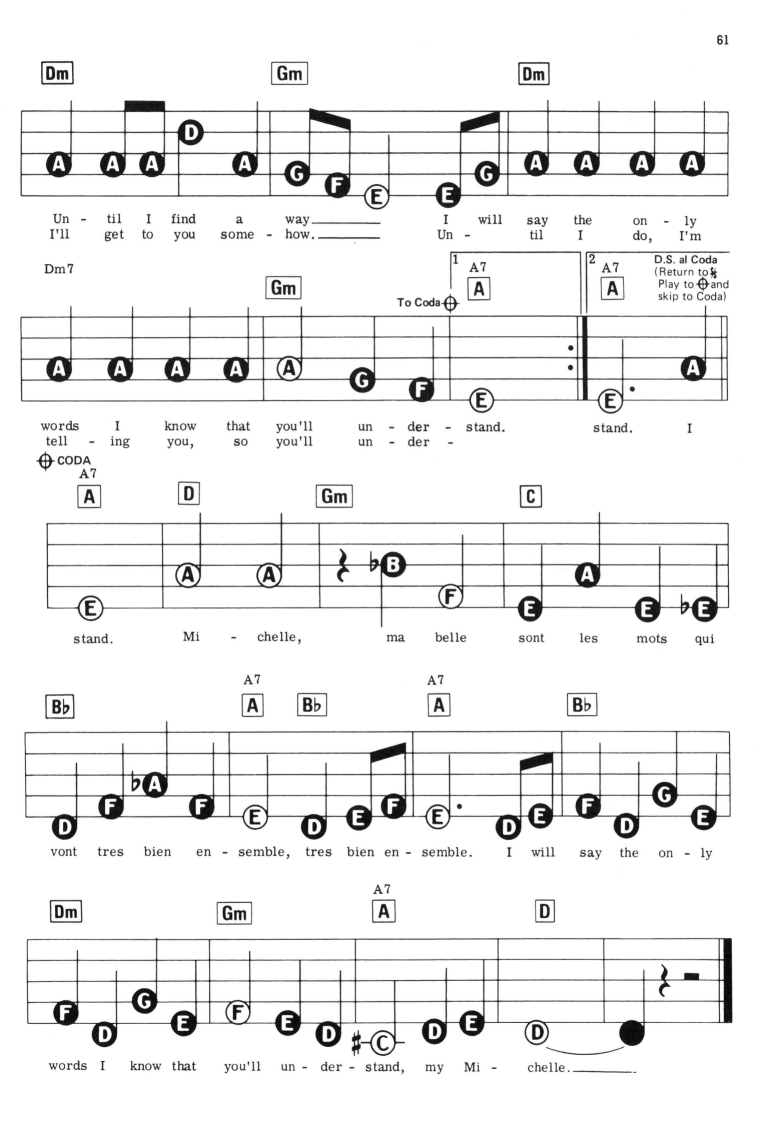

Mother Nature's Son

Registration 4
Rhythm: 8 Beat or Rock

Words and Music by John Lennon
and Paul McCartney

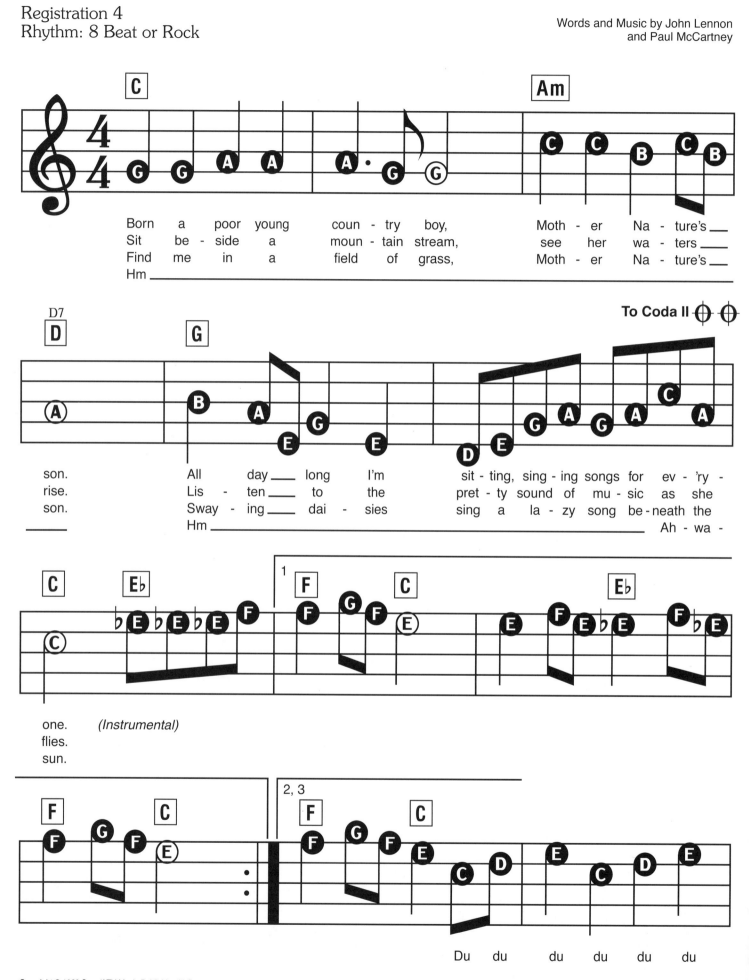

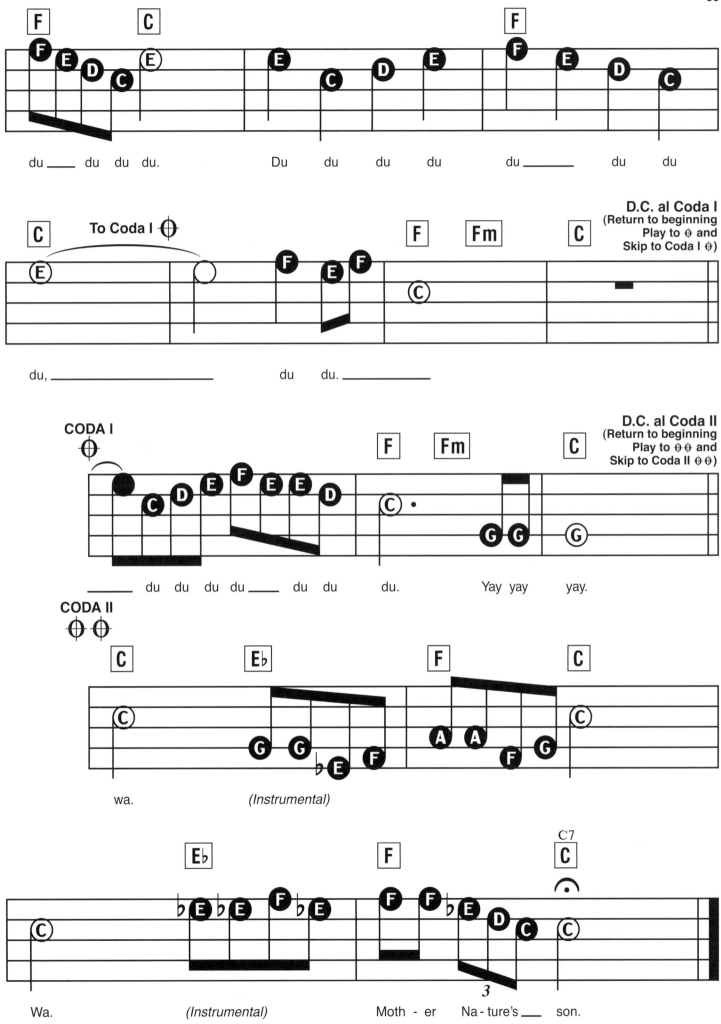

Nowhere Man

Registration 2
Rhythm: Rock

Words and Music by John Lennon
and Paul McCartney

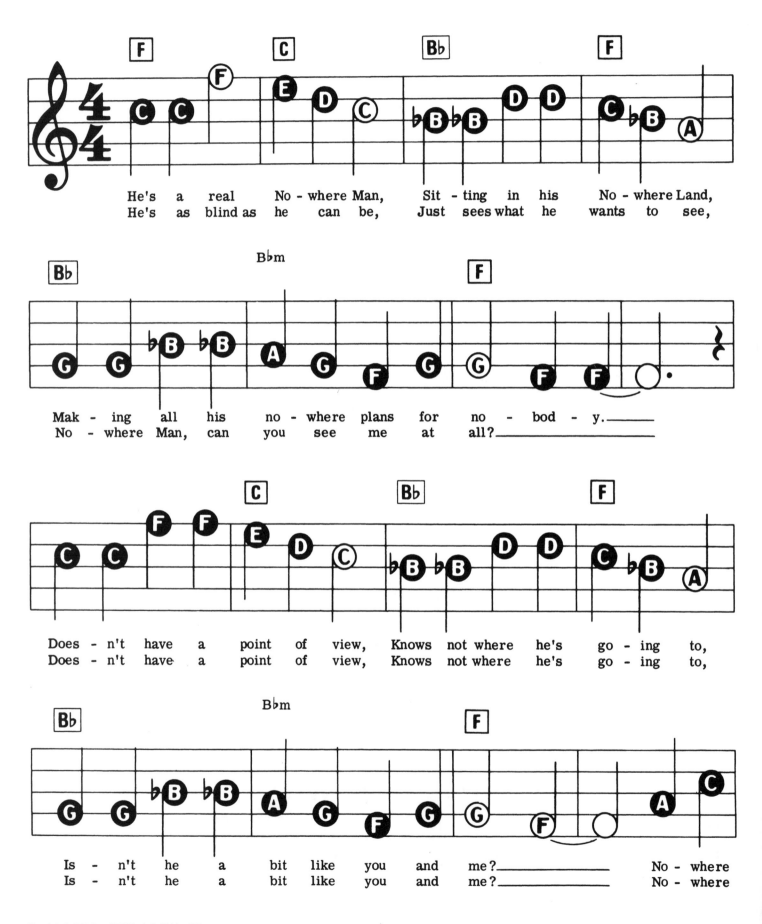

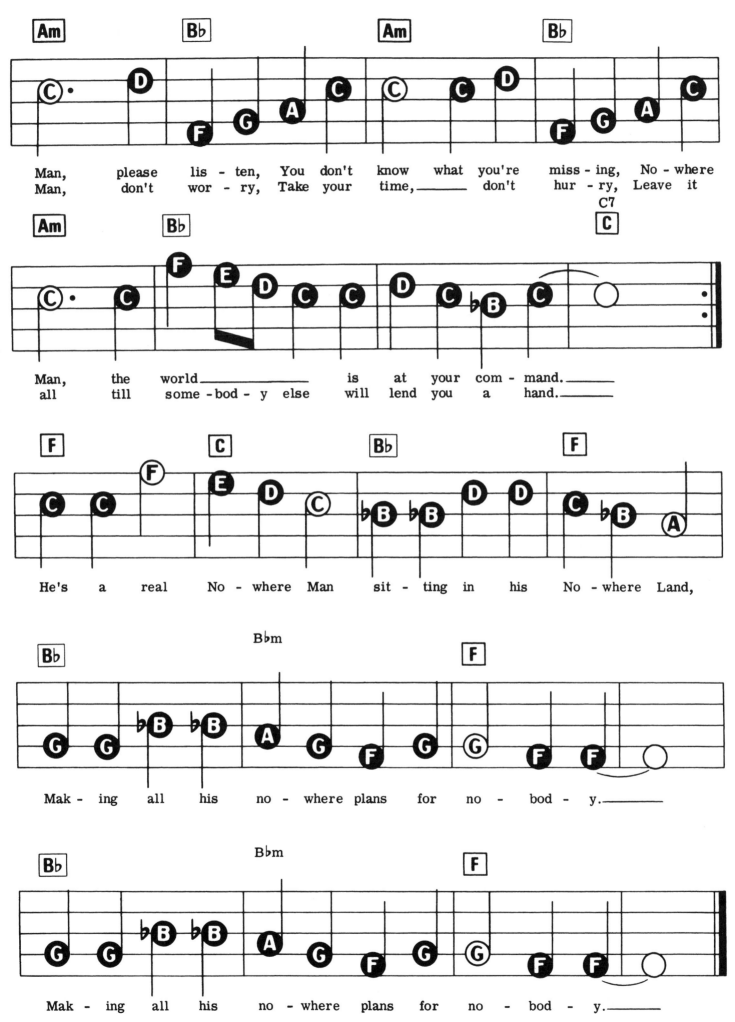

Ob-La-Di, Ob-La-Da

Registration 9
Rhythm: Rock

Words and Music by John Lennon
and Paul McCartney

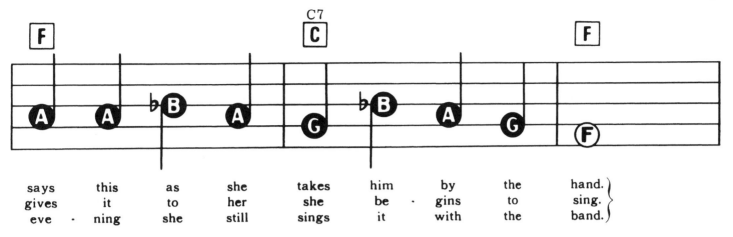

says this as she takes him by the hand.
gives it to her she be · gins to sing.
eve · ning she still sings it with the band.

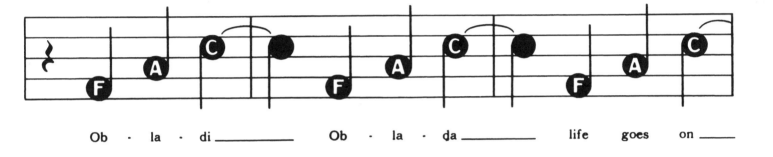

Ob · la · di _____ Ob · la · da _____ life goes on _____

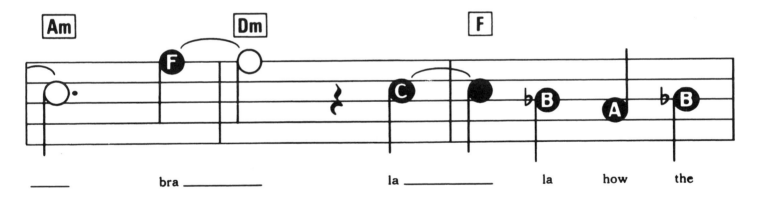

_____ bra _____ la _____ la how the

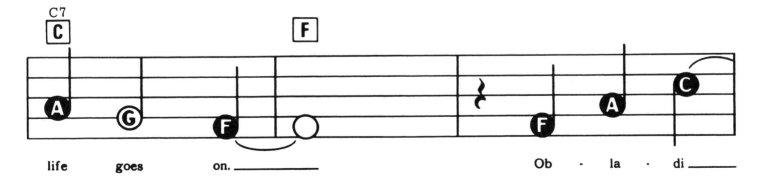

life goes on. _____ Ob · la · di _____

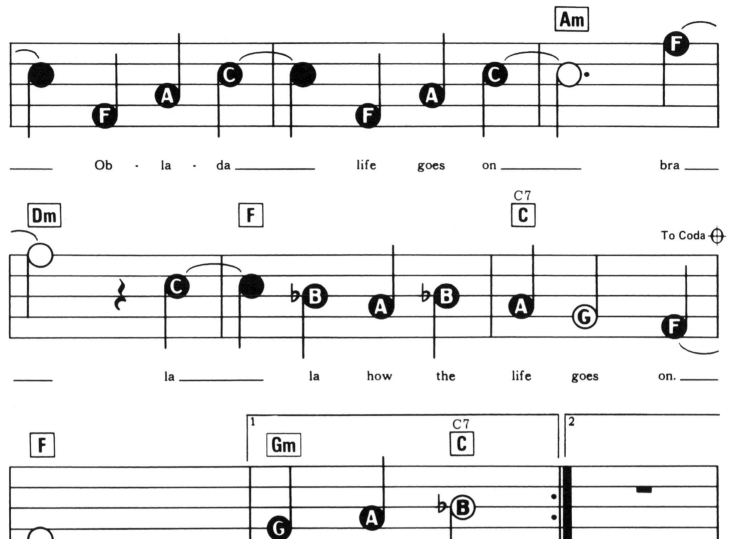

Ob · la · da _____ life goes on _____ bra _____

la _____ la how the life goes on. _____

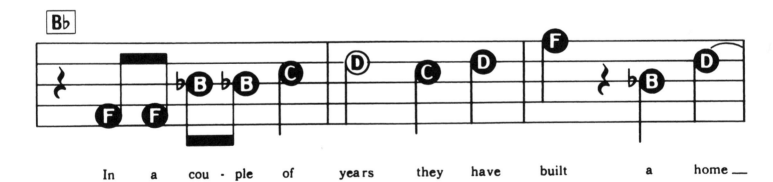

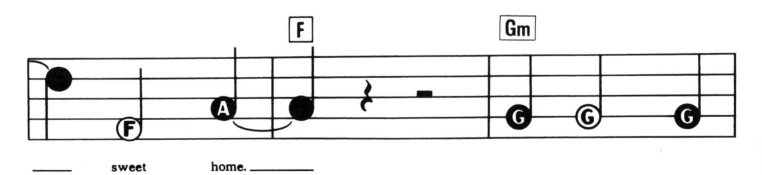

In a cou · ple of years they have built a home _____

sweet home. _____

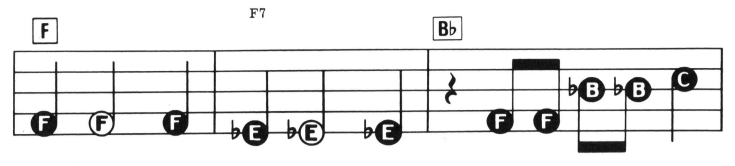

With a cou - ple of

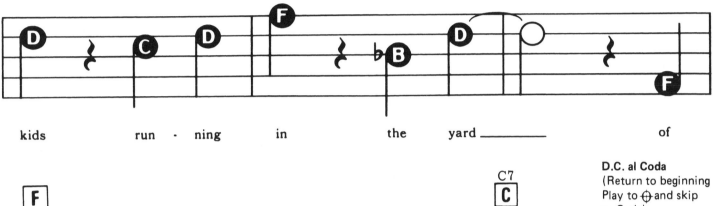

kids run - ning in the yard _____ of

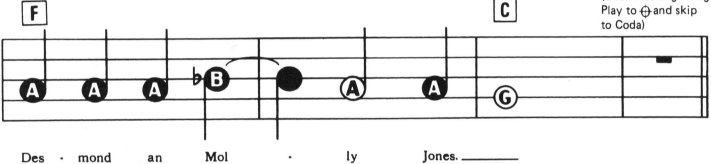

Des - mond an Mol - ly Jones. _____

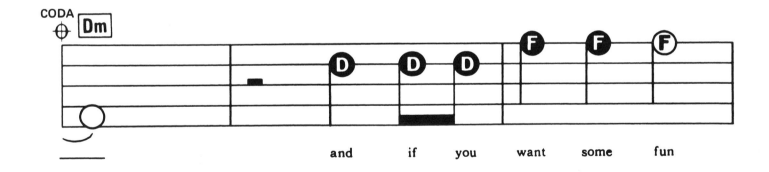

and if you want some fun

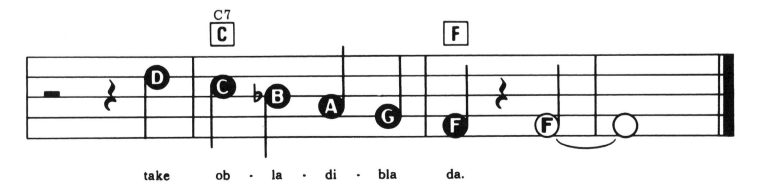

take ob - la - di - bla da.

Penny Lane

Registration 2
Rhythm: Rock

Words and Music by John Lennon
and Paul McCartney

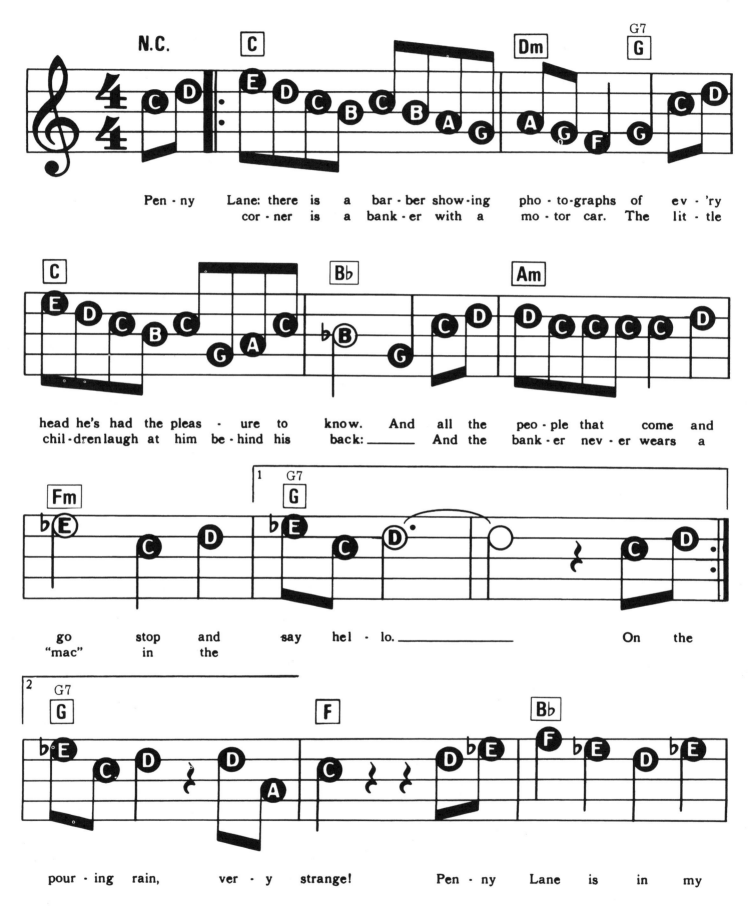

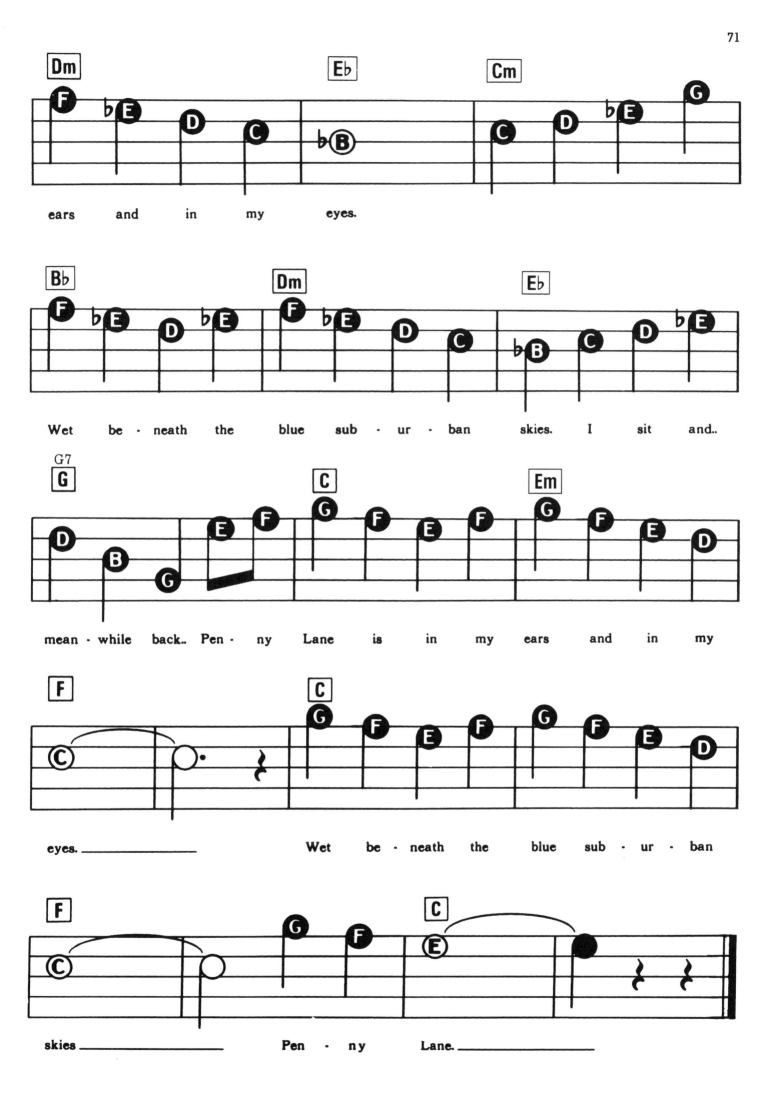

Please Please Me

Registration 8
Rhythm: Rock

Words and Music by John Lennon
and Paul McCartney

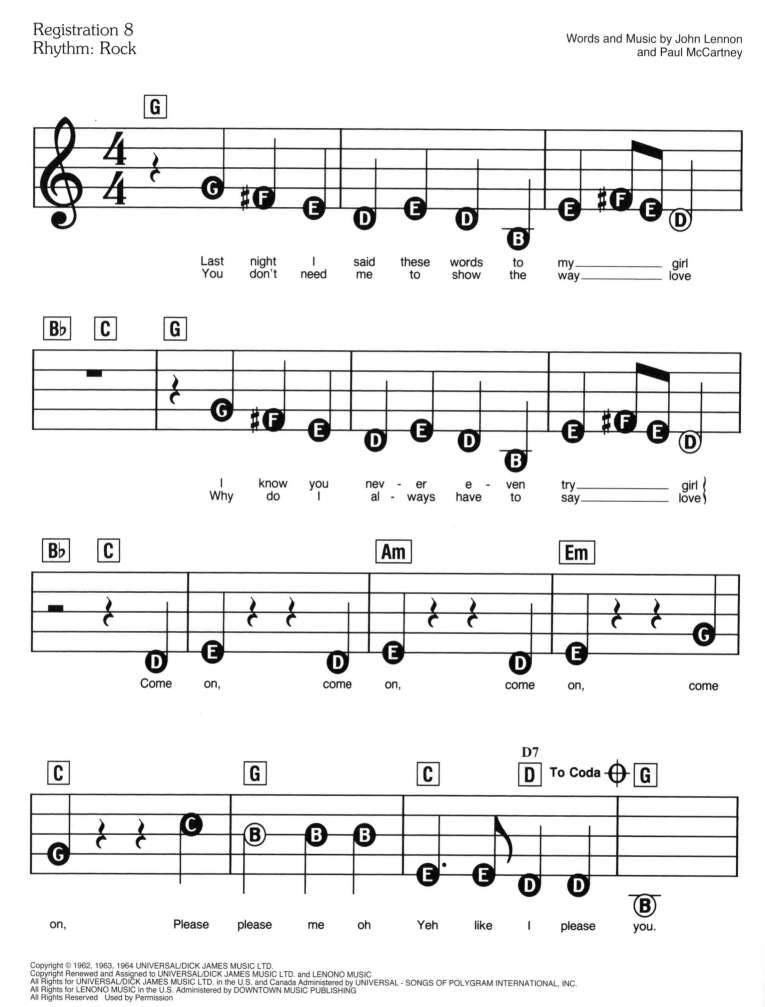

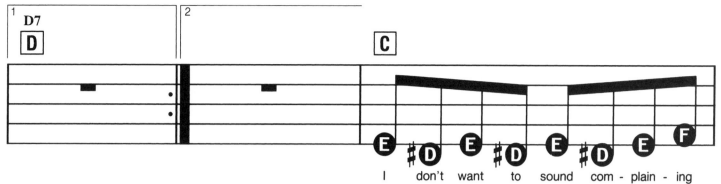

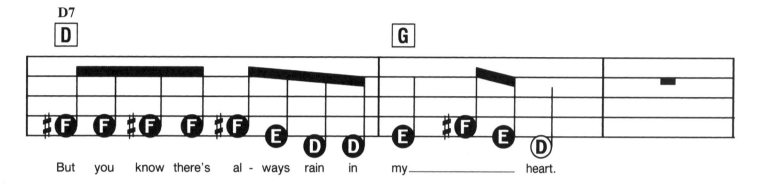

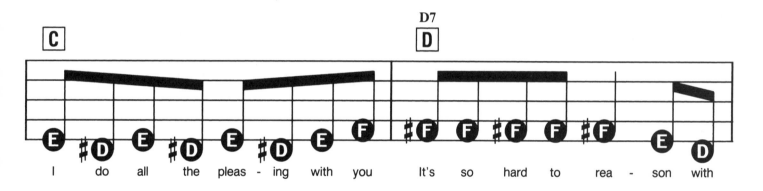

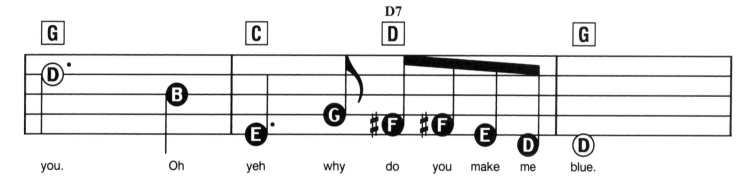

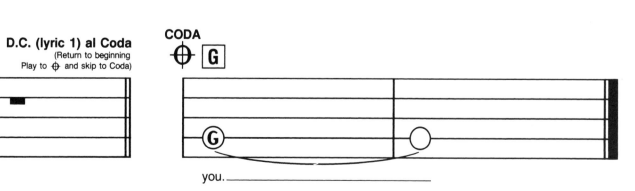

Sgt. Pepper's Lonely Hearts Club Band

Registration 4
Rhythm: Rock

Words and Music by John Lennon
and Paul McCartney

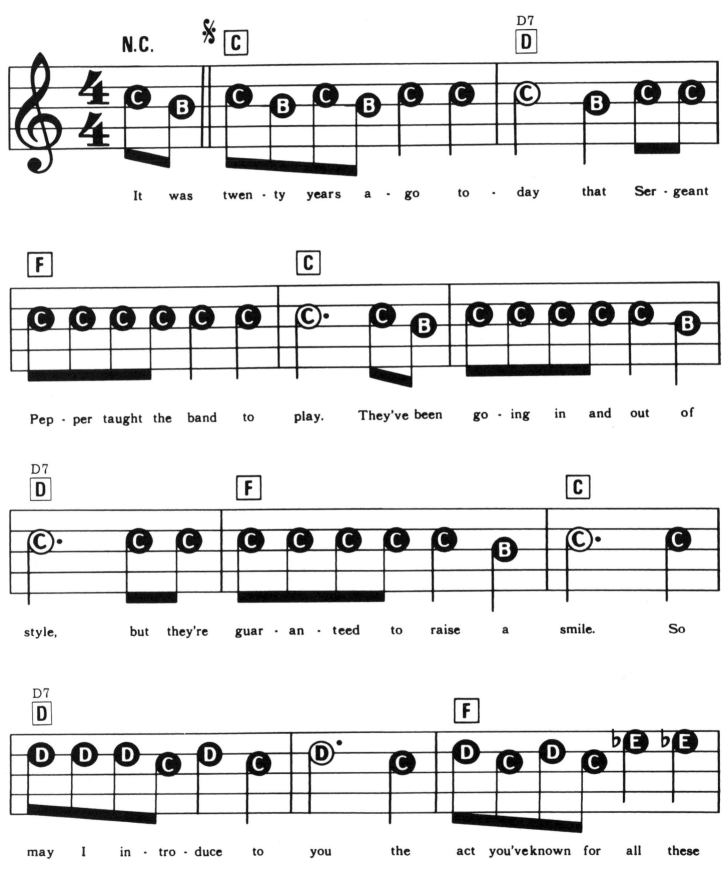

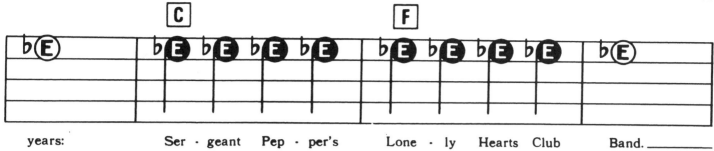

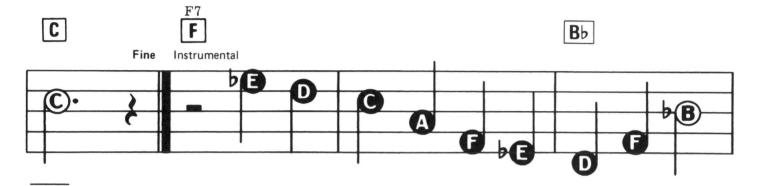

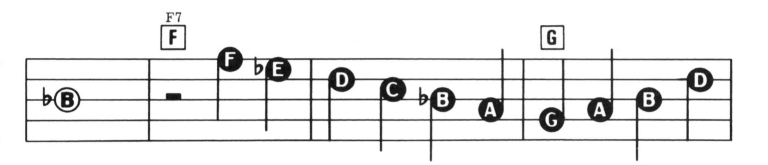

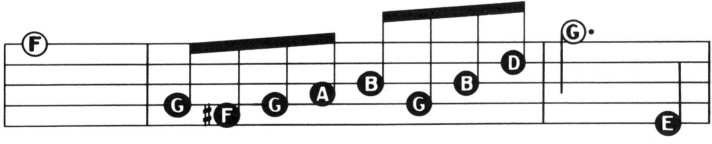

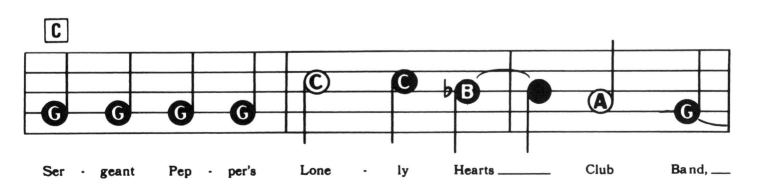

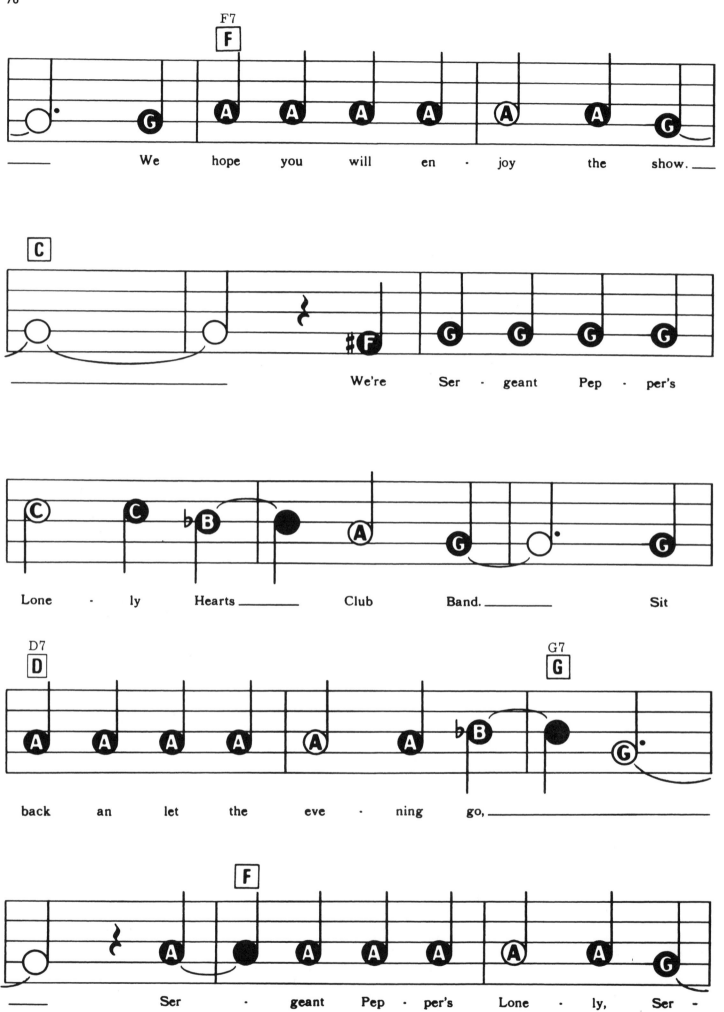

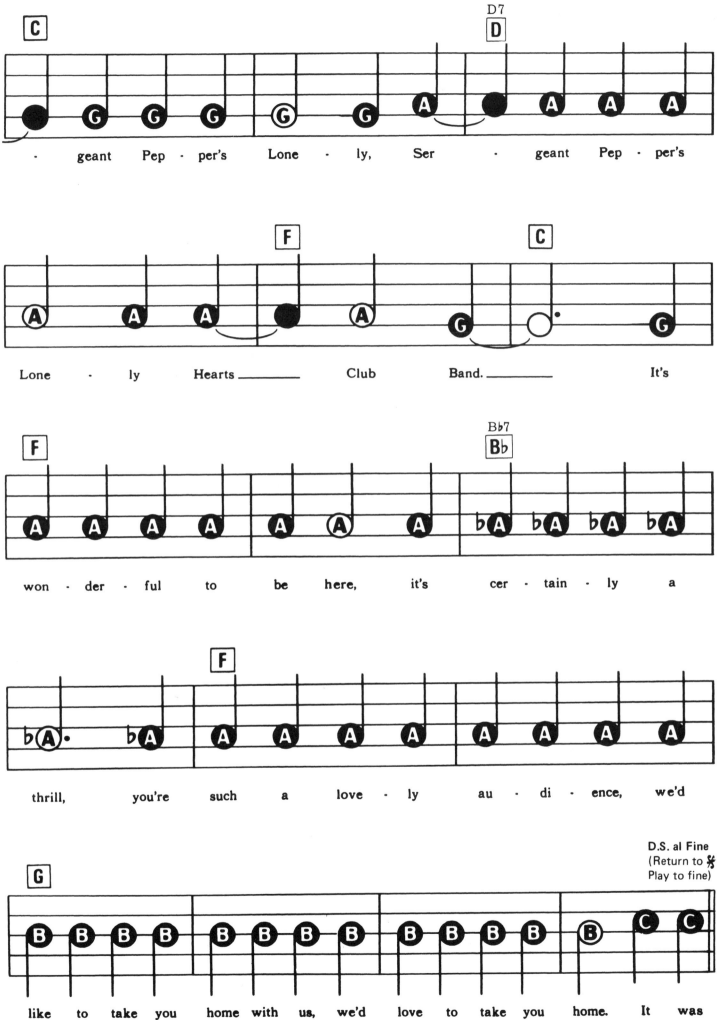

Sexy Sadie

Registration 4
Rhythm: Rock or 8-Beat

Words and Music by John Lennon
and Paul McCartney

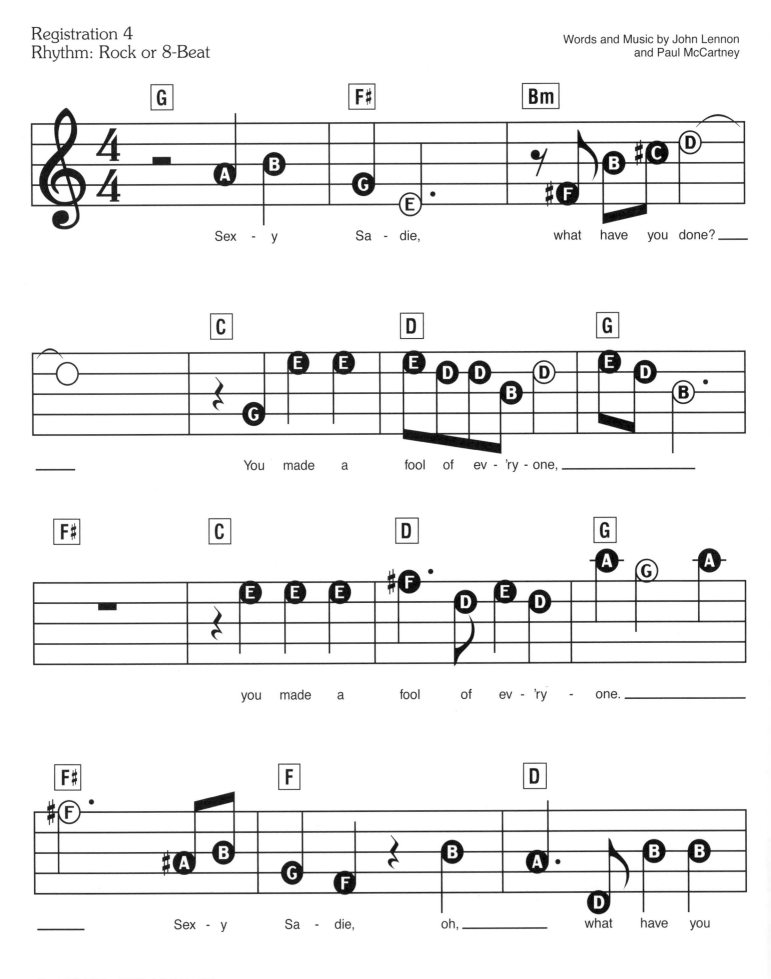

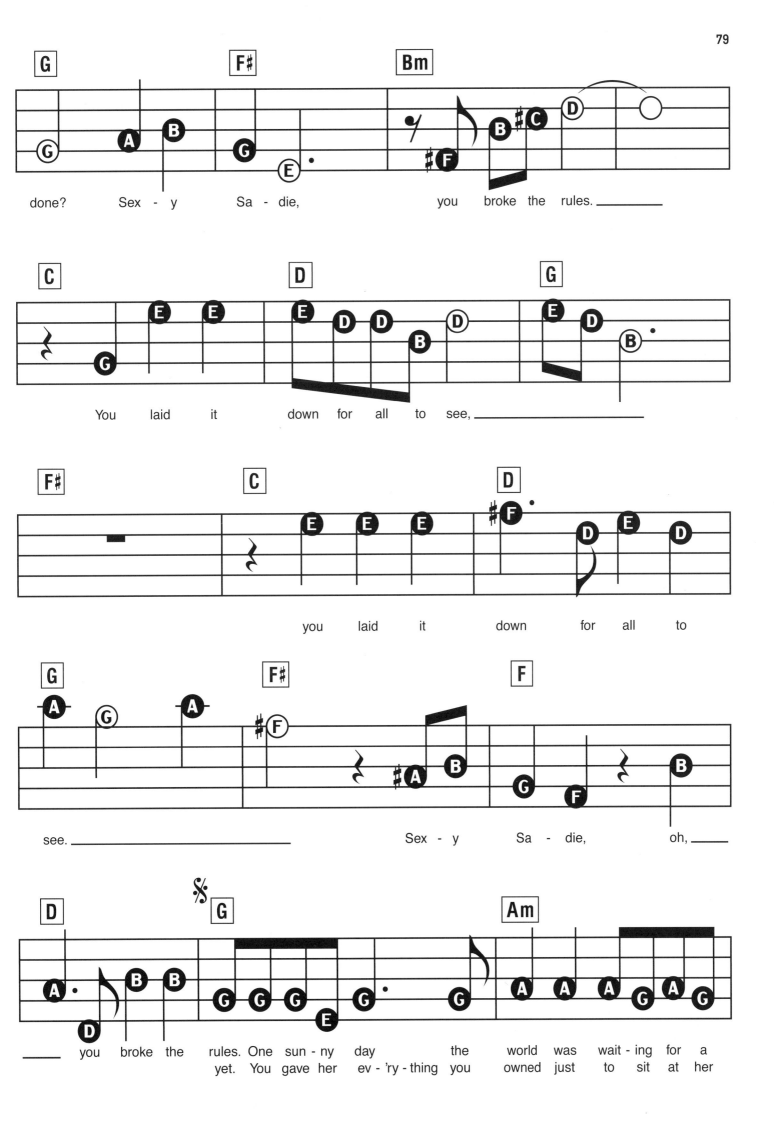

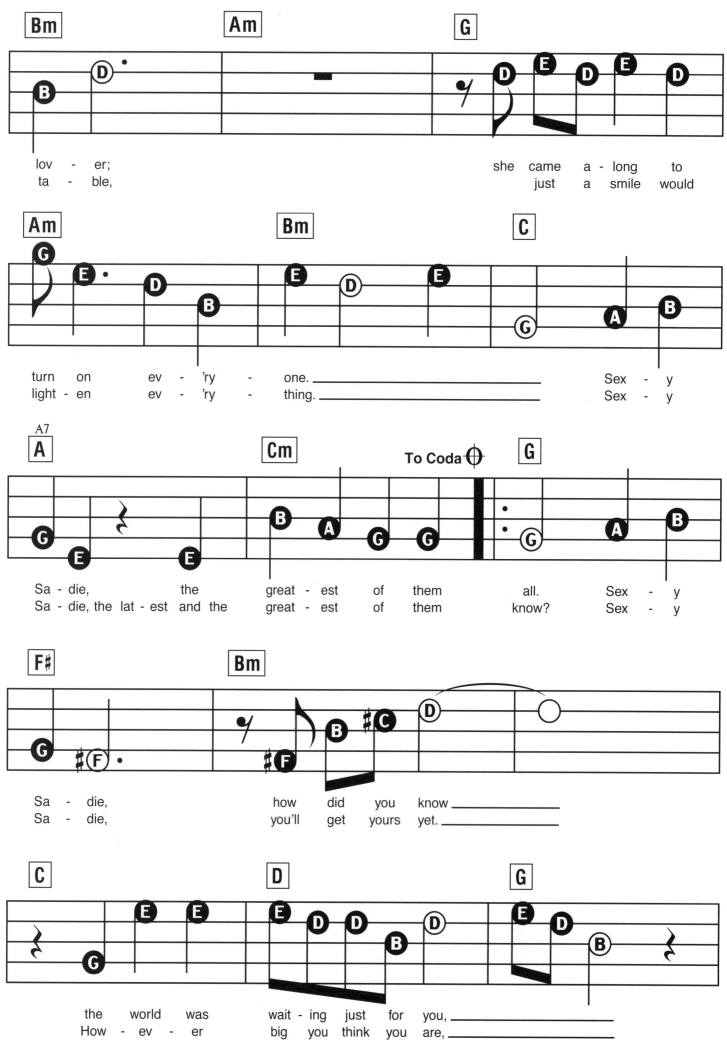

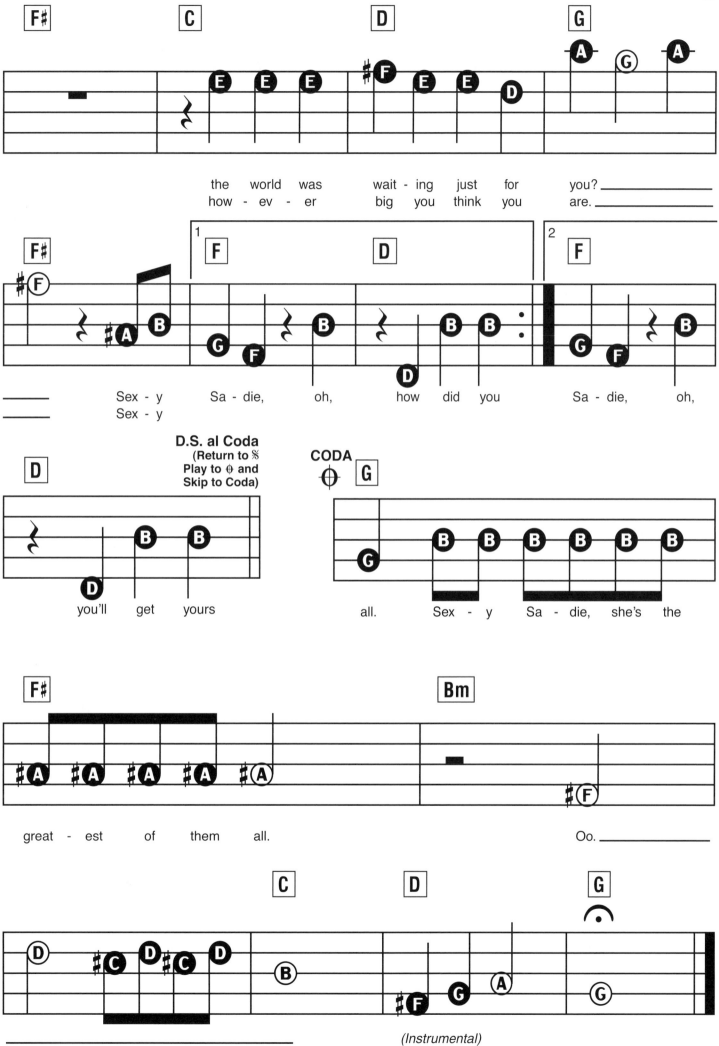

the world was wait - ing just for you? _____
how - ev - er big you think you are. _____

_____ Sex - y Sa - die, oh, how did you Sa - die, oh,
_____ Sex - y

D.S. al Coda
(Return to %
Play to ⊕ and
Skip to Coda)

you'll get yours

CODA

all. Sex - y Sa - die, she's the

great - est of them all. Oo. _____

_____ (Instrumental)

She Came in Through the Bathroom Window

Registration 4
Rhythm: Rock or 8-Beat

Words and Music by John Lennon
and Paul McCartney

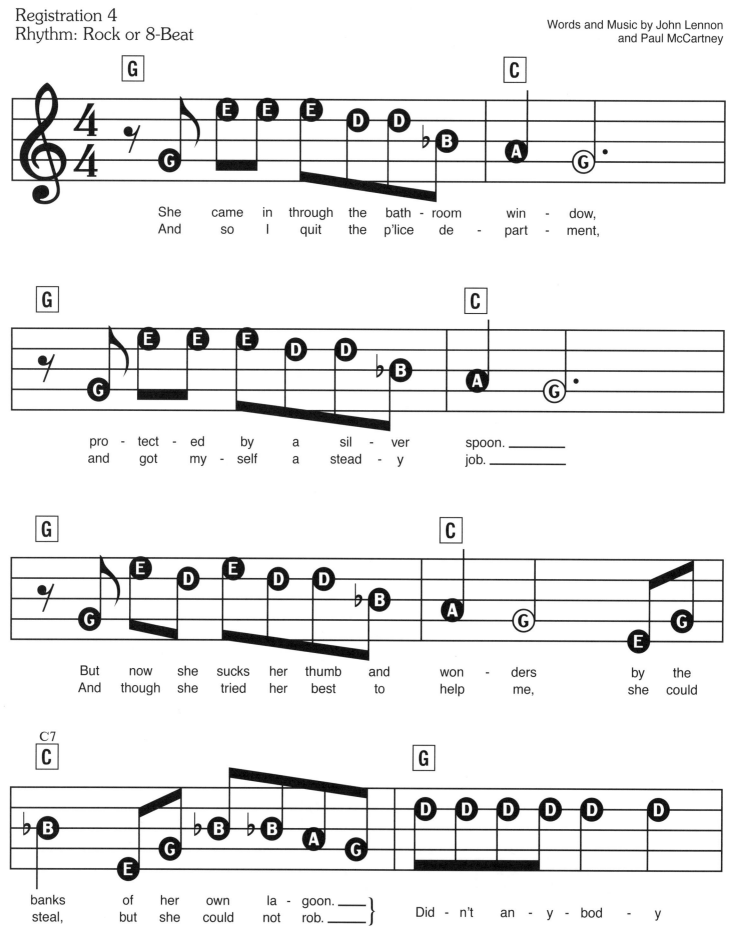

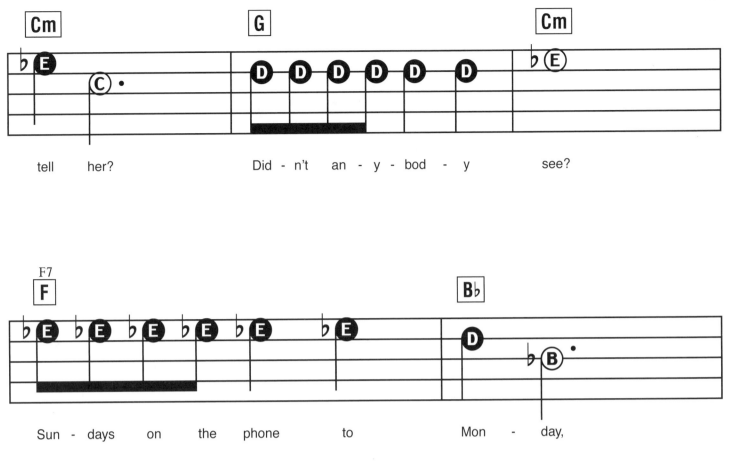

tell her?   Did - n't an - y - bod - y   see?

Sun - days   on   the   phone   to   Mon -   day,

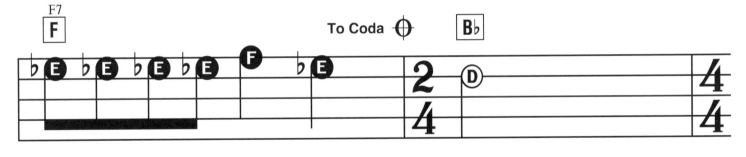

Tues - days   on   the   phone   to   me.

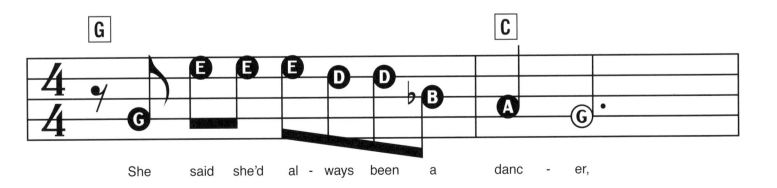

She   said she'd al - ways been   a   danc - er,

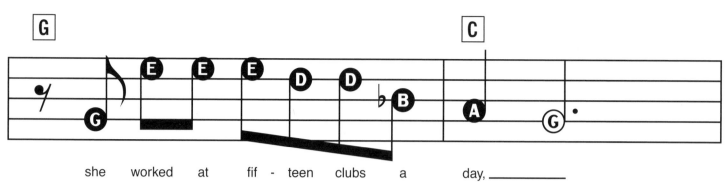

she worked at fif - teen clubs a day, _____

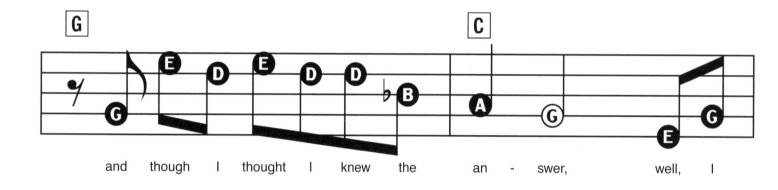

and though I thought I knew the an - swer, well, I

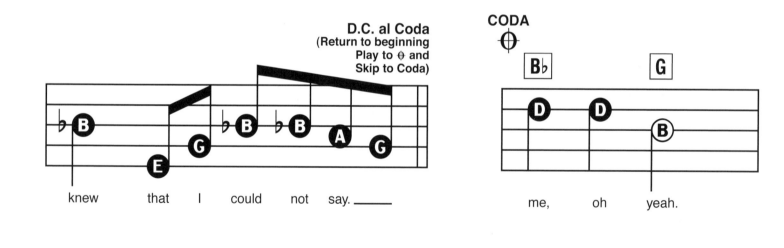

D.C. al Coda
(Return to beginning
Play to ⊕ and
Skip to Coda)

CODA

knew that I could not say. _____

me, oh yeah.

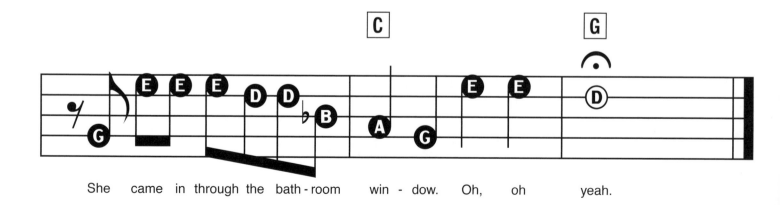

She came in through the bath - room win - dow. Oh, oh yeah.

Strawberry Fields Forever

Registration 2
Rhythm: Rock

Words and Music by John Lennon
and Paul McCartney

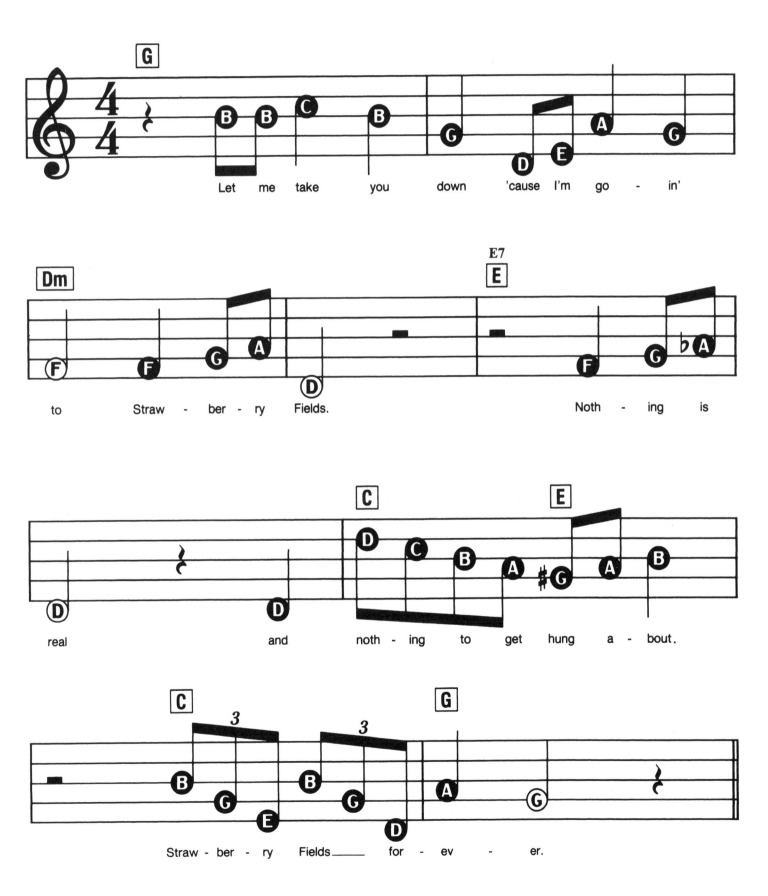

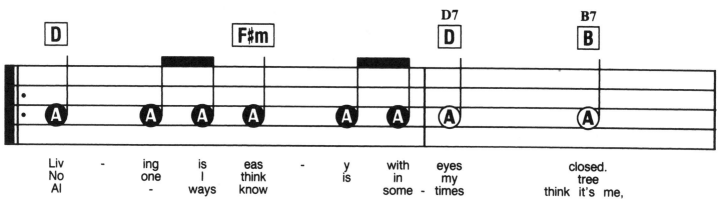

Liv - ing is eas - y with eyes closed.
No one I think is in my tree
Al - ways know sometimes think it's me,

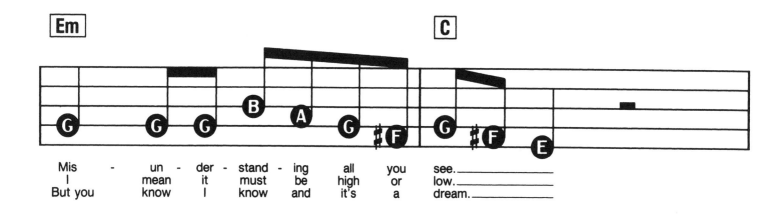

Mis - un - der - stand - ing all you see.____
I mean it must be all high or low.____
But you know I know and it's a dream.____

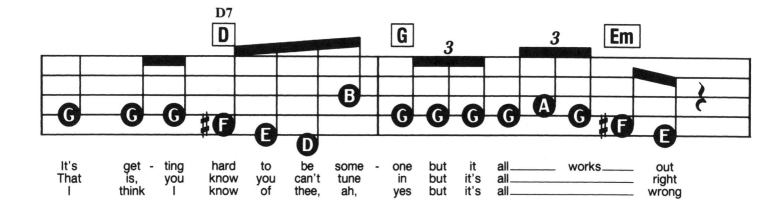

It's get - ting hard to be some - one but it all____ works____ out
That is, you know you can't tune in, but it's all____ right
I think I know of thee, ah, yes but it's all____ wrong

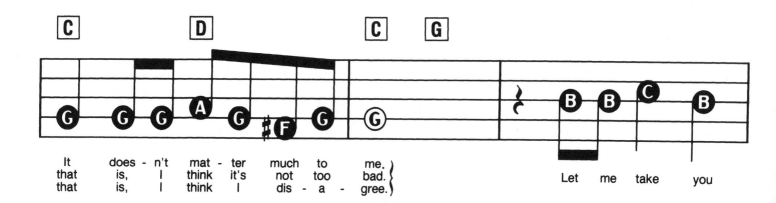

It does - n't mat - ter much to me.
that is, I think it's not too bad.
that is, I think I dis - a - gree.

Let me take you

87

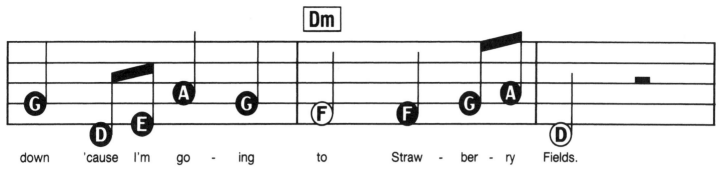

down 'cause I'm go - ing   to   Straw - ber - ry Fields.

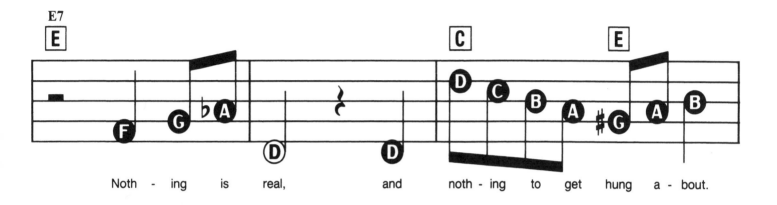

Noth - ing is real,   and noth - ing to get hung a - bout.

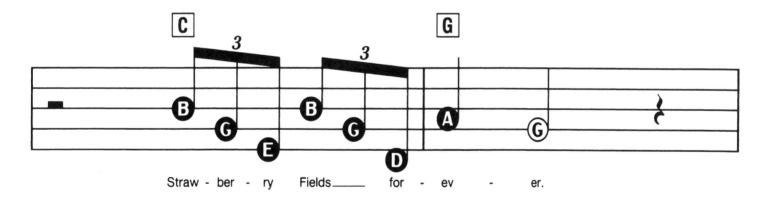

Straw - ber - ry Fields___ for - ev - er.

Repeat and Fade

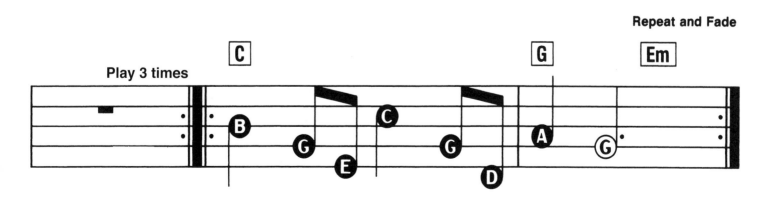

Play 3 times

Ticket to Ride

Registration 4
Rhythm: Rock

Words and Music by John Lennon
and Paul McCartney

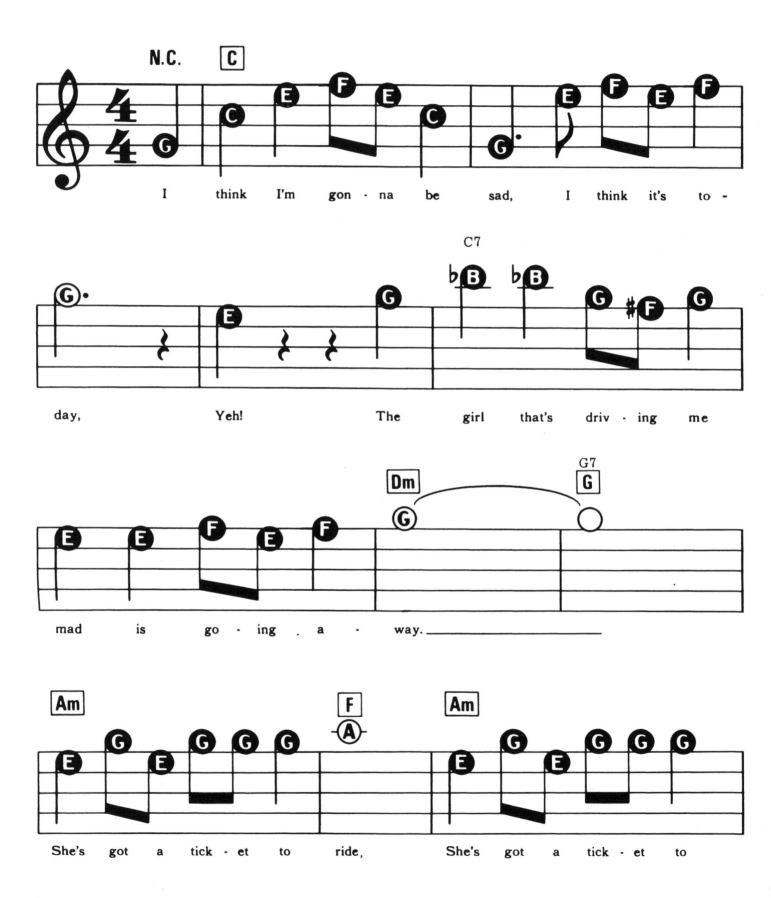

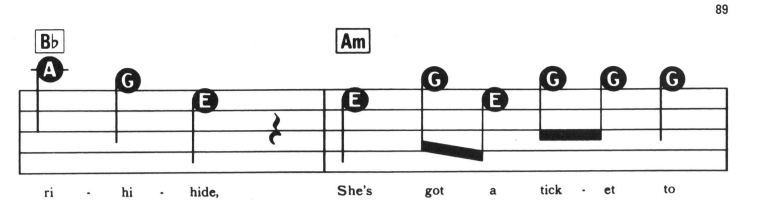

ri - hi - hide, She's got a tick - et to

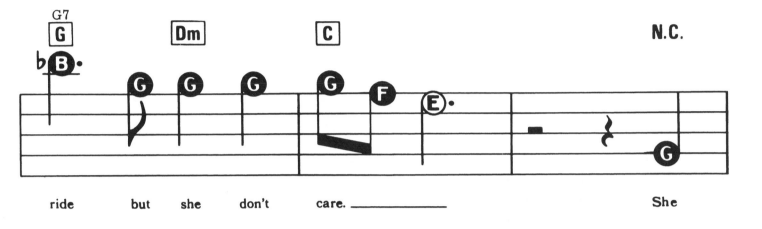

ride but she don't care. _____ She

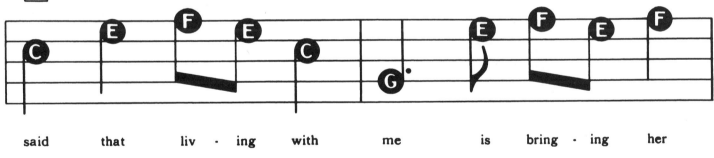

said that liv - ing with me is bring - ing her

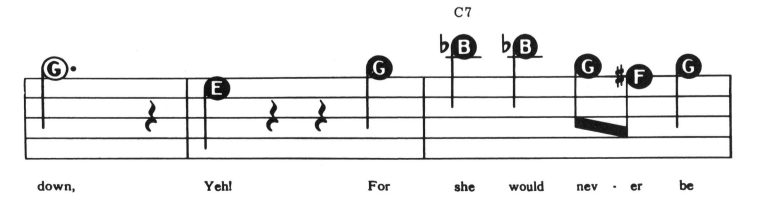

down, Yeh! For she would nev - er be

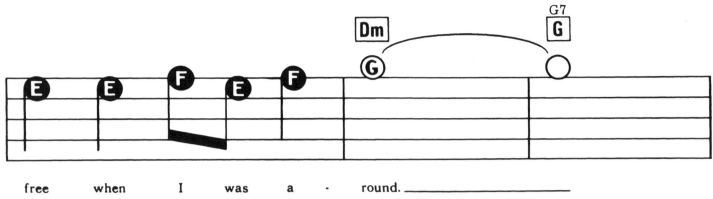

free   when   I   was   a - round. _____

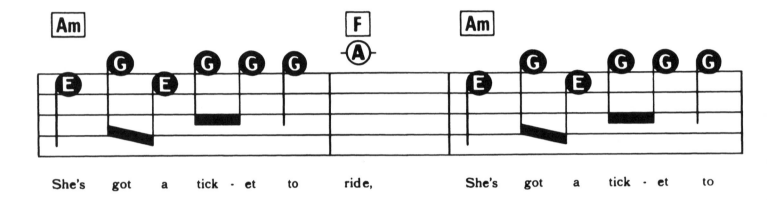

She's   got   a   tick - et   to   ride,   She's   got   a   tick - et   to

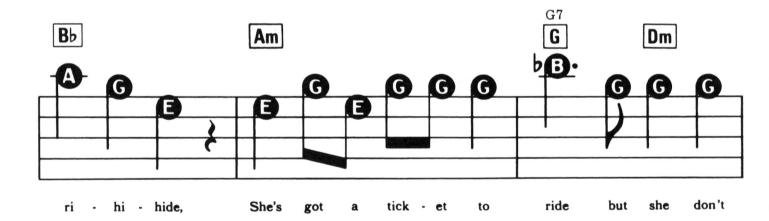

ri - hi - hide,   She's   got   a   tick - et   to   ride   but   she   don't

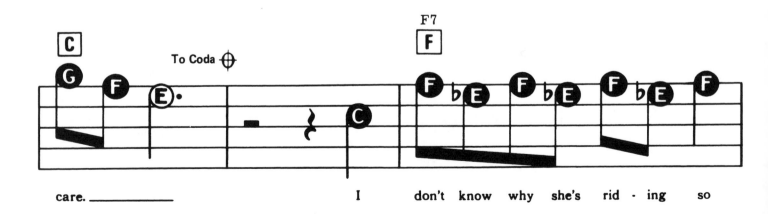

care. _____   I   don't   know   why   she's   rid - ing   so

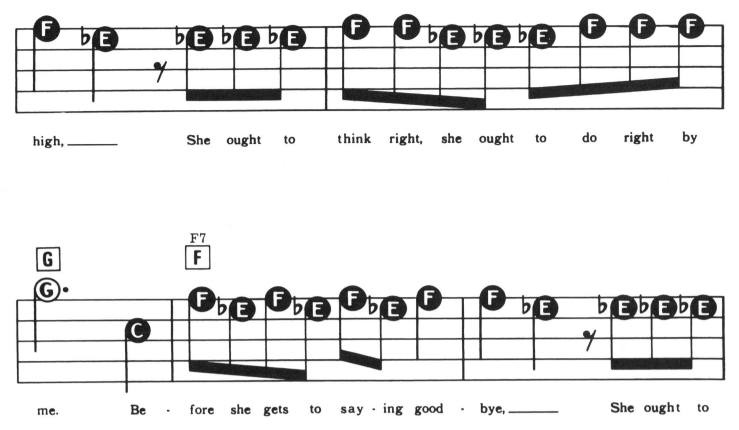

high, _____ She ought to think right, she ought to do right by

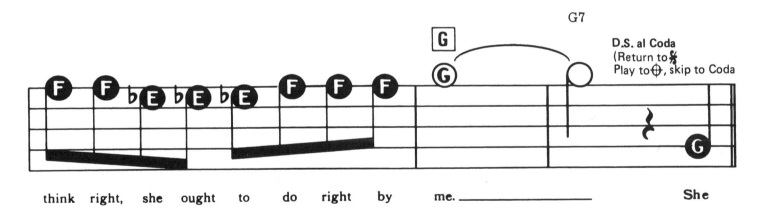

me. Be - fore she gets to say - ing good - bye, _____ She ought to

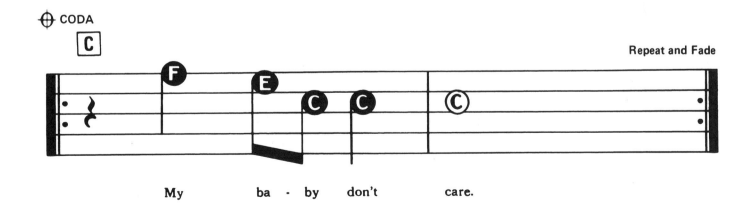

think right, she ought to do right by me. _____ She

My ba - by don't care.

We Can Work It Out

Registration 9
Rhythm: Rock

Words and Music by John Lennon
and Paul McCartney

Try to see it my way, Do I have to keep on talk-ing till I can't go on?

To Coda

While you see it your way, Run the risk of know-ing that our love may soon be gone.

We can work it out. We can work it out. _____ Think of what you're say - ing,

You can get it wrong and still you think that it's all right.

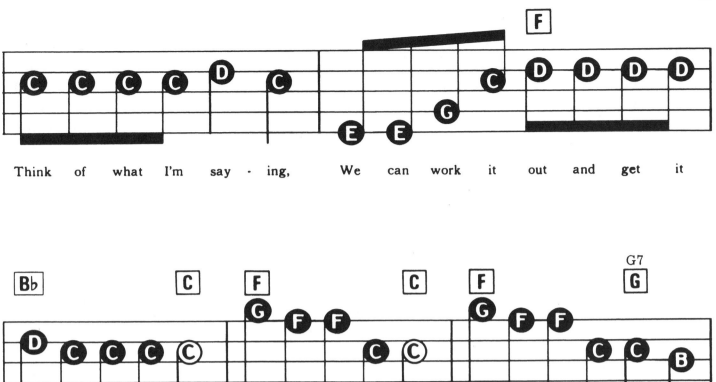

Think of what I'm say - ing, We can work it out and get it

straight, or say good-night. We can work it out. We can work it out. _____

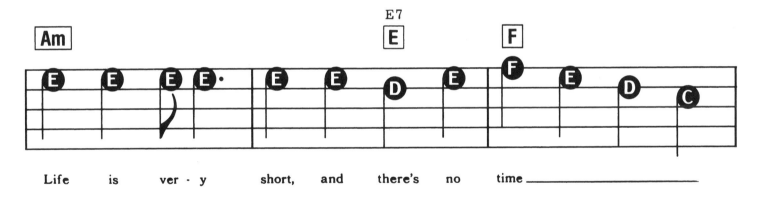

Life is ver - y short, and there's no time _____

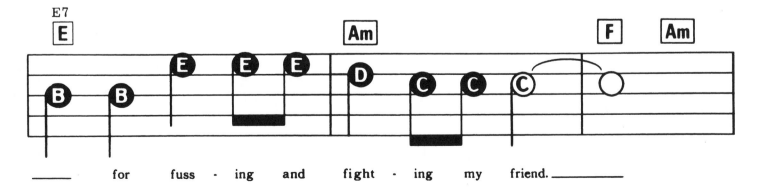

_____ for fuss - ing and fight - ing my friend. _____

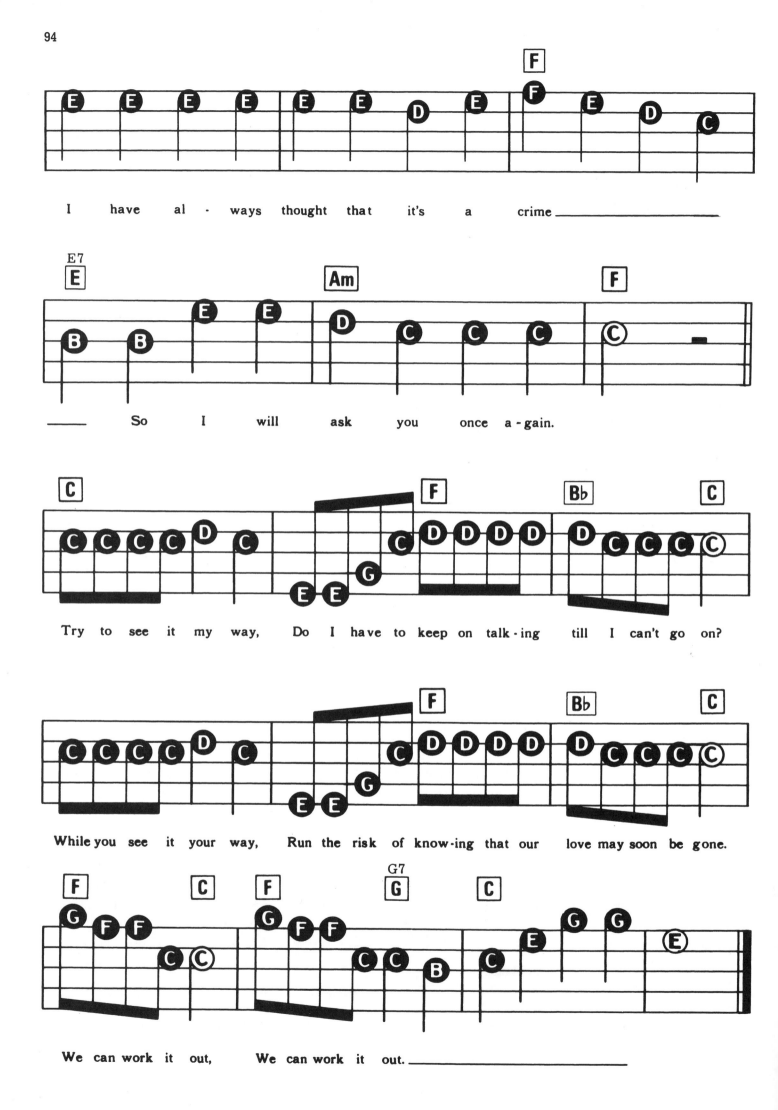

With a Little Help from My Friends

Registration 5
Rhythm: Swing or Shuffle

Words and Music by John Lennon
and Paul McCartney

C **G** **Dm**

E F G G F E D E F F F F

What would you do if I sang out of tune would you

G7
G **C** **G**

E D D D C D E E F G G F E

stand up and walk out on me. Lend me your ears and I'll

Dm **G7** **G** **C**

D E F F F F E D D D C D E C G E

sing you a song and I'll try not to sing out of key Oh, I get

Bb **F** **C**

D C C C C C C C C G C E

by with a lit-tle help from my friends Mm, I get

96

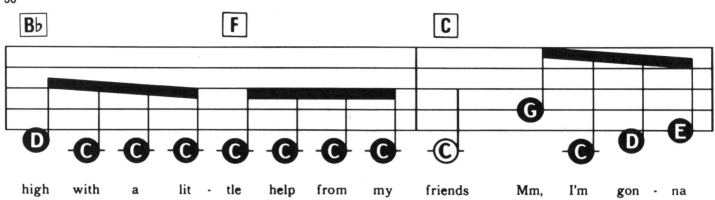

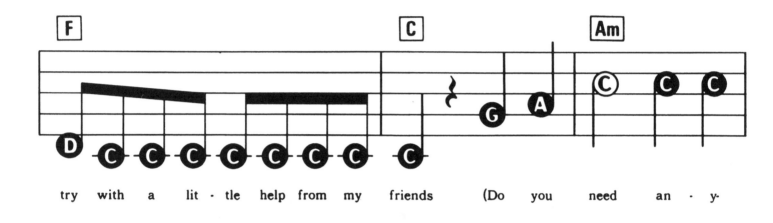

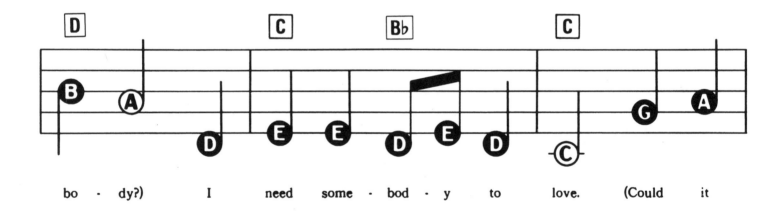

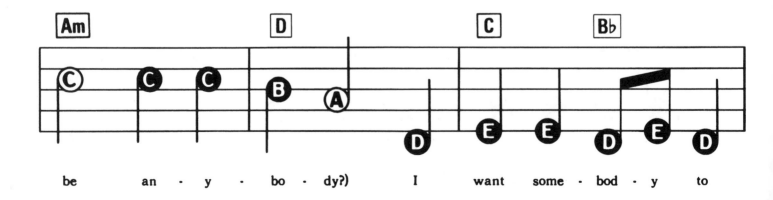

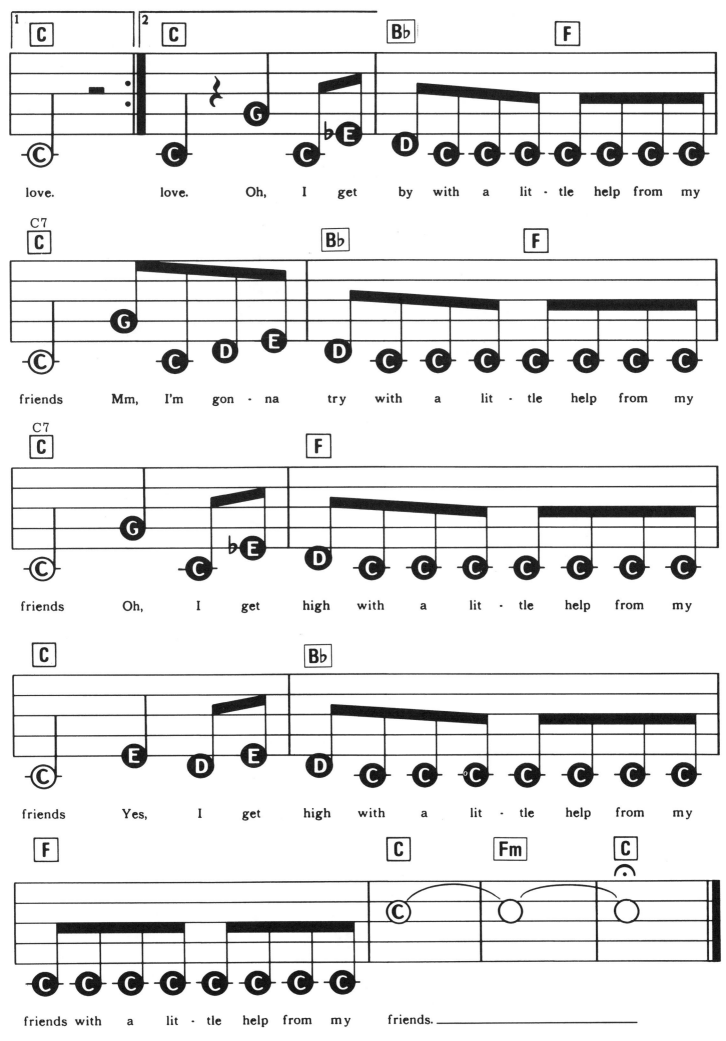

love. love. Oh, I get by with a lit-tle help from my

friends Mm, I'm gon-na try with a lit-tle help from my

friends Oh, I get high with a lit-tle help from my

friends Yes, I get high with a lit-tle help from my

friends with a lit-tle help from my friends.

Yellow Submarine

Registration 2
Rhythm: 8-Beat or Rock

Words and Music by John Lennon
and Paul McCartney

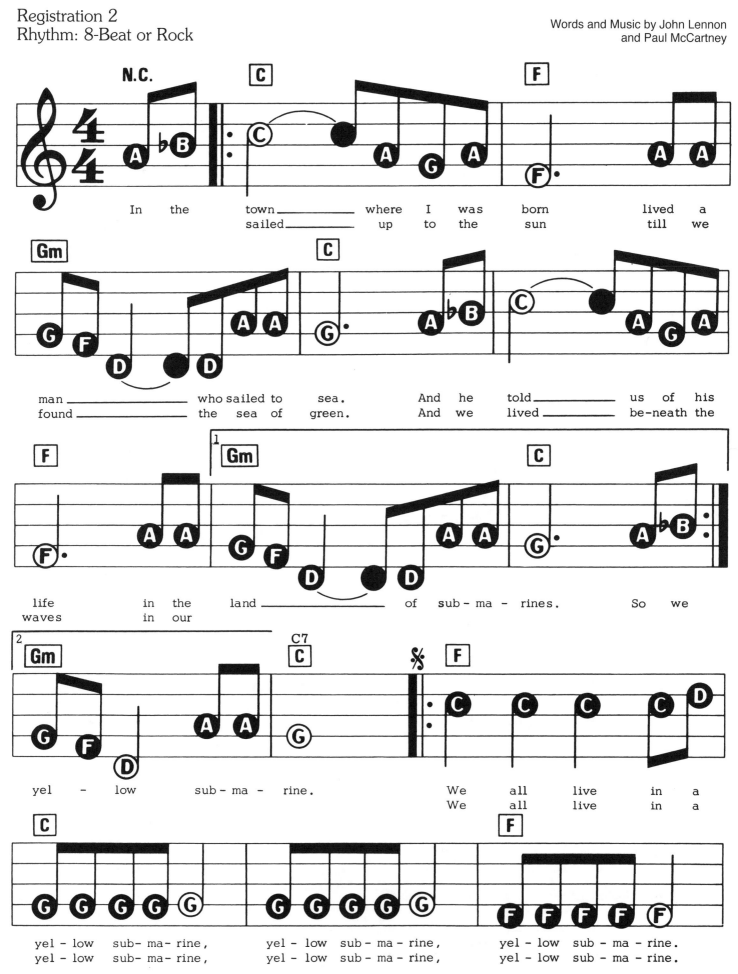

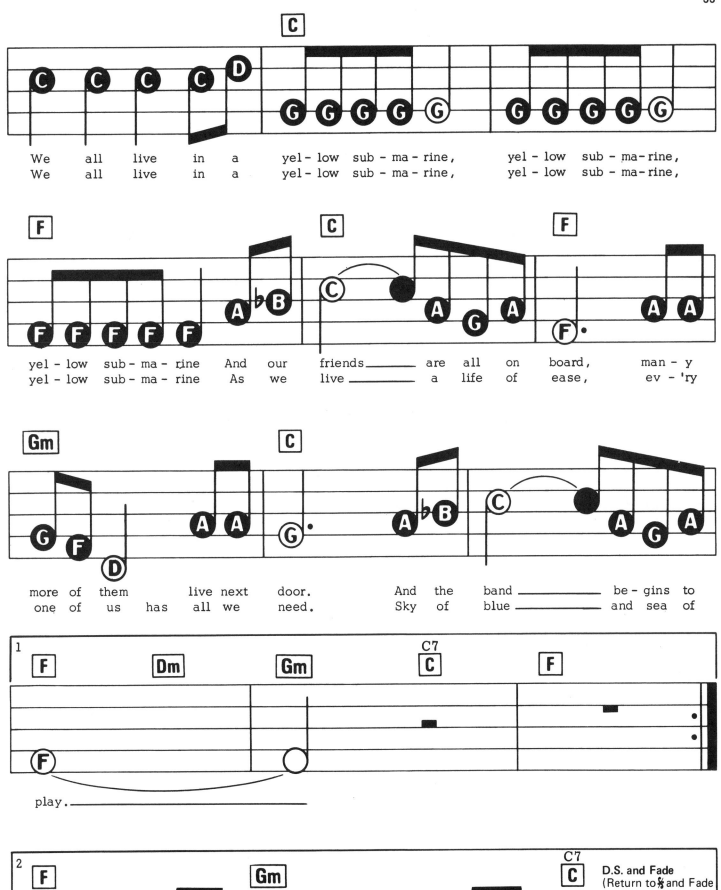

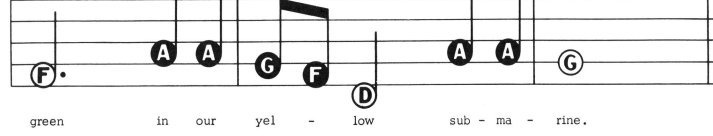

Yesterday

Registration 2
Rhythm: Rock or Ballad

Words and Music by John Lennon
and Paul McCartney

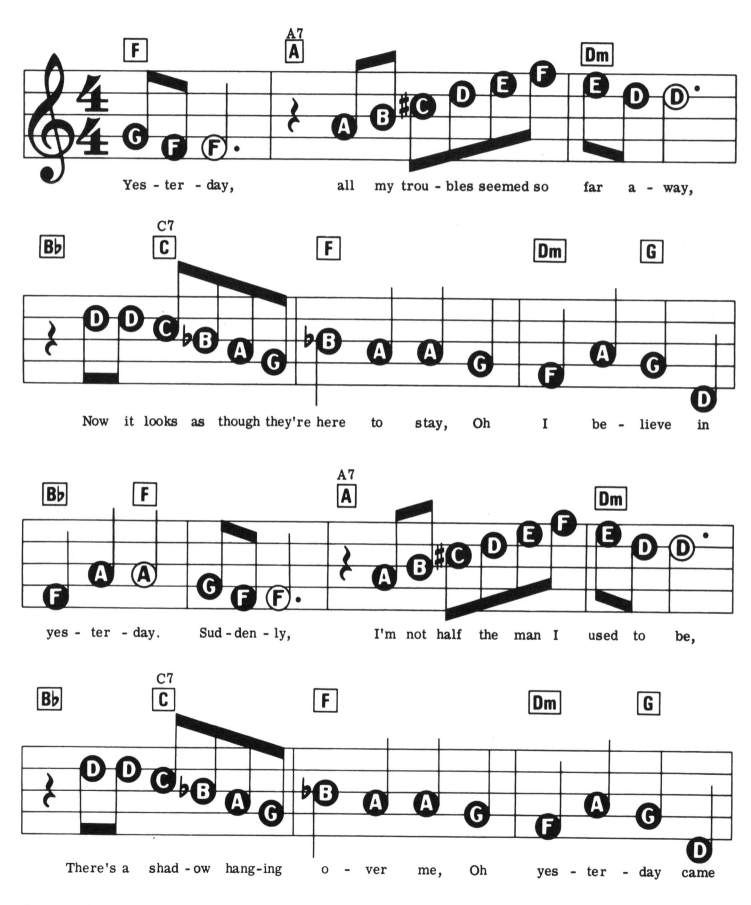

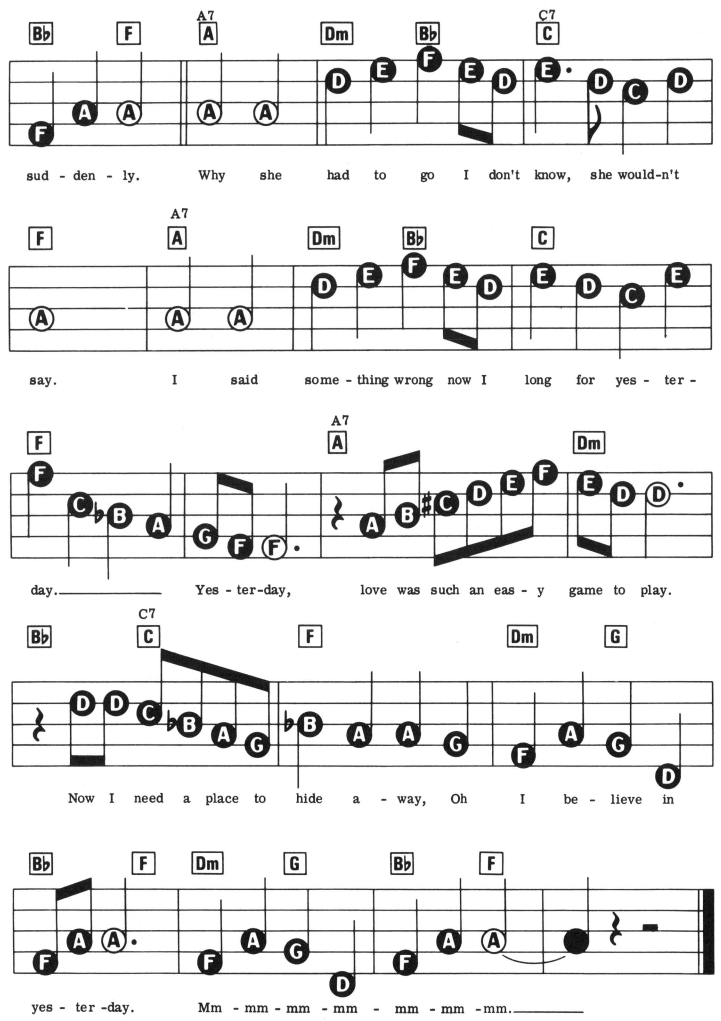

Your Mother Should Know

Registration 2
Rhythm: Rock or Shuffle

Words and Music by John Lennon
and Paul McCartney

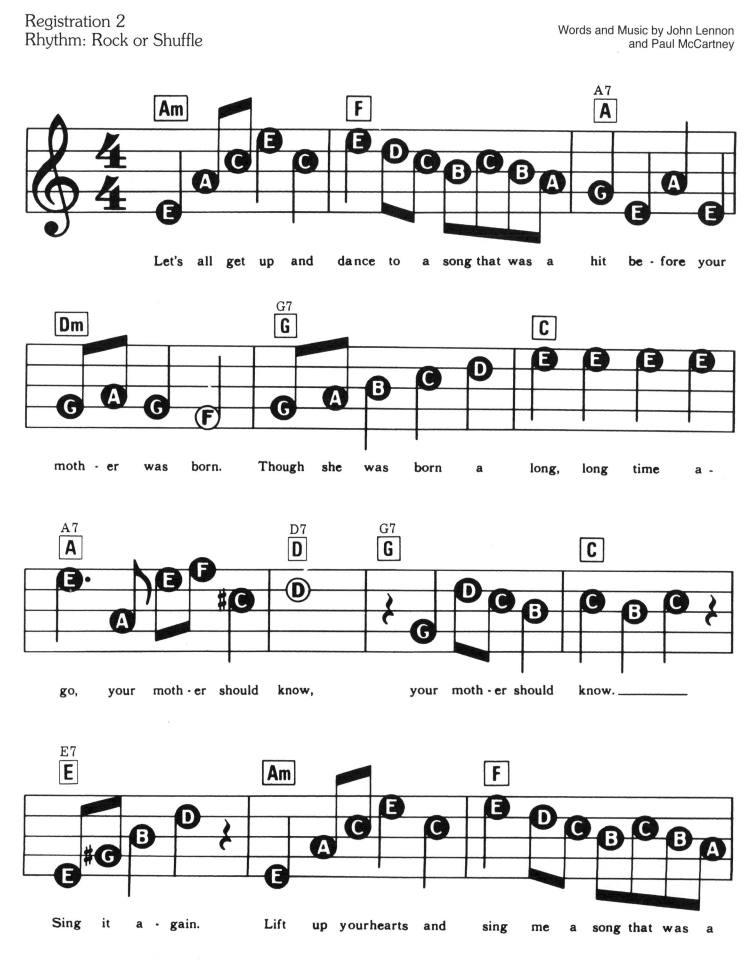

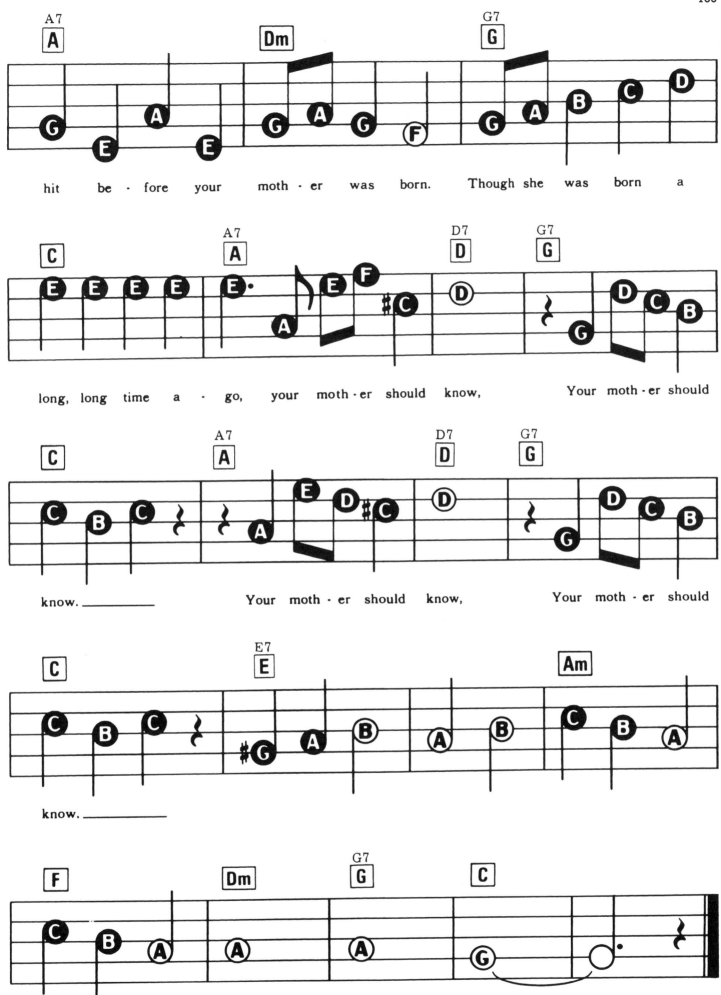

Registration Guide

• Match the Registration number on the song to the corresponding numbered category below. Select and activate an instrumental sound available on your instrument.

• Choose an automatic rhythm appropriate to the mood and style of the song. (Consult your Owner's Guide for proper operation of automatic rhythm features.)

• Adjust the tempo and volume controls to comfortable settings.

Registration

1	Mellow	Flutes, Clarinet, Oboe, Flugel Horn, Trombone, French Horn, Organ Flutes
2	Ensemble	Brass Section, Sax Section, Wind Ensemble, Full Organ, Theater Organ
3	Strings	Violin, Viola, Cello, Fiddle, String Ensemble, Pizzicato, Organ Strings
4	Guitars	Acoustic/Electric Guitars, Banjo, Mandolin, Dulcimer, Ukulele, Hawaiian Guitar
5	Mallets	Vibraphone, Marimba, Xylophone, Steel Drums, Bells, Celesta, Chimes
6	Liturgical	Pipe Organ, Hand Bells, Vocal Ensemble, Choir, Organ Flutes
7	Bright	Saxophones, Trumpet, Mute Trumpet, Synth Leads, Jazz/Gospel Organs
8	Piano	Piano, Electric Piano, Honky Tonk Piano, Harpsichord, Clavi
9	Novelty	Melodic Percussion, Wah Trumpet, Synth, Whistle, Kazoo, Perc. Organ
10	Bellows	Accordion, French Accordion, Mussette, Harmonica, Pump Organ, Bagpipes